A Hillbilly:

His Search for the Correct Path

Published by James E. Gibson, Freelance Writer
Lexington, KY

James E. Gibson

A Hillbilly: His Search for the Correct Path

Copyright © 2020 by James E. Gibson

All Rights Reserved. No part of this book may be reproduced or transmitted in any form or by any means without written permission from the copyright owner, James E. Gibson, with the exception of brief quotes that are considered "fair use" under copyright law.

ISBN: 978-0-9988774-3-3
LCCN: 2020904796

Published September 30, 2020, with numerous small changes/corrections made in October 2020

Published by James E. Gibson, Freelance Writer
P.O. Box 54868, Lexington, KY 40555-4868
United States of America
Email: jamesegibson@gmail.com

You may contact the author at the address above. He appreciates all comments, questions, suggestions, etc., but cannot promise to provide everyone a personal reply.

Even if in quotation marks, all "quotations" in the book should be considered paraphrases due to my limited memory of the exact original statements.

Most of the contents of this book are being first published in the book. However, some contents are reprinted and/or adapted from material the author has previously published elsewhere in print and/or online.

Table of Contents

Acknowledgments 4

About the Front Cover 5

Disclaimer 6

Chapter 1: Introduction and Early Years 7

Chapter 2: Growing Up, Early Grade School Years 22

Chapter 3: Middle Elementary School Years at Stone ... 41

Chapter 4: Finishing Grade School and High School 70

Chapter 5: My College Years and Early "Career" Years 87

Chapter 6: Living in Nicholasville, Then Back in Jenkins 107

Chapter 7: Back in Lexington 115

Chapter 8: My Writing 120

Chapter 9: The Future and Closing Thoughts 133

About the Author 138

Order Form and Ordering Information 139

Acknowledgments

The highest righteous power, which I call God, deserves credit and glory for any good from this book. Without God I could do nothing, wouldn't even exist.

Thanks also to all my relatives, friends, neighbors, coworkers, and everyone else that I've encountered in my life for their help. They have helped me immensely in various ways over the years of my life thus far.

These individuals are too numerous to mention specifically by name. In fact, to help prevent persons from getting undesired publicity, I seldom mention names and specific personal information in the book. However, I love everyone and appreciate the positive roles everyone has played in my life.

Thank you all very much!

About the Front Cover

White symbolizes purity and unity. The white cover contains every color of the rainbow. The colored vertical lines symbolize some of the various paths I could take with my life. They also add color to the cover. The white vertical line at the center symbolizes the straight, correct path, which I seek to adhere to.

I like to think I chose a simple, plain path instead of the bright lights of the limelight, despite the garish bright colors on my book's front cover.

The colored horizontal lines represent diversity and add more color to the cover. The blue book title symbolizes the heavens, sky, and God. The green subtitle and author name symbolize human greenness, limited knowledge.

The simple cover I created (under God's leadership I hope) saved me the expense of hiring a professional cover designer—and enabled me to create the cover my (God's?) way

Disclaimer

I believe everything I wrote in this book is true. Furthermore, I tried to present the truth without hyperbole, which I consider a fancy word for lying.

Most of the book is based on my personal memories. I sought to be accurate and to present things honestly in a relatively positive way. God deserves the credit to the extent that I succeeded. However, errors could occur due to my misunderstanding events originally when they happened, faulty personal memory, or errors in my writing.

In cases where my descriptions are not based on my personal memory, but are events described to me by someone else or that I learned about through research of some type, errors could also occur due to incorrect information from my source(s) for whatever reason(s).

This autobiography omits some things due to limited space and omits others to avoid embarrassment to various persons (including me!). The book is certainly not a comprehensive description of my life. It emphasizes my childhood and things that progressed me further along my path toward being a writer.

All the opinions expressed in this book are those of the author (me, James E. Gibson). They do not reflect the views of any other person or organization.

I love everyone and hope nothing I've written offends anyone.

Chapter 1: Introduction and Early Years

This story is only my story. It is not typical of hillbillies' stories, because each of us is different.

Due to my dad being college educated, owning many books, and subscribing to several magazines and newspapers, I got exposure to a lot of stuff that many don't. Of course, I also lack the mechanical skills and dexterity that many hillbillies have.

People like to stereotype hillbillies. But there is not one type of hillbilly. Hillbillies come rich and poor, black and white, old and young, college educated and elementary school dropouts, drug addicts and abstainers who don't use tobacco, alcohol, or illegal drugs. Some are skilled laborers, others are general laborers.

Two Past Bestsellers About Hillbillies

My autobiography is a personal story. This book lacks the research of and offers a different perspective from that of J. D. Vance's 2016 book that became a bestseller, *Hillbilly Elegy: A Memoir of a Family and Culture in Crisis*. I read his book, and found some of it insightful, but I felt he was overly pessimistic and one-sided. But that's just my view.

My book also lacks the depth of *Night Comes to the Cumberlands: A Biography of a Depressed Area*, Harry M. Caudill's bestseller from the early 1960s about the plight of persons in southeastern Kentucky. Again, my book is more optimistic than Caudill's.

Both those earlier books contain many truths,

brought out via significant research and personal experience. But they only tell part of the story. Each of us hillbillies has our own story. And there are significant strengths and benefits to growing up in the mountains of southeastern Kentucky. I'm proud to call myself a hillbilly in the good sense of the term.

Though I doubt my autobiography will ever become a bestseller, I feel it has a place. My original plans were to have the word "hillbilly" in the title of my first book, *True Christianity: It May Not Be What You Think*, published in 2014 (second edition 2015, third edition 2017). But I changed the focus of that book. Therefore, I changed the working title and the final title of it before finishing and publishing it.

My Birth

I was born in the Benham Hospital in Benham. Benham is a small coal mining town in Harlan County in southeastern Kentucky. It is in the Appalachian Mountains area, making me a hillbilly.

My dad and mom moved from the Benham Hotel (which mom and dad described as being a far cry from what we normally think of today as a hotel) in Benham, Kentucky to an apartment in Lynch, Kentucky on Saturday, February 1st, 1958 according to mom. I was born on Monday, February 3, 1958 at the Benham Hospital. Mom told me that I was due February 5th, 1958.

She said the doctor asked if they still lived at the Benham Hotel. When mom told him they'd moved, he said "That's why that baby came early" according to mom.

My Grandparents, Mom's Side of the Family

My two sets of grandparents illustrate some of the differences between my parents' families. My maternal grandparents had little formal education. Mom said her mom only went to the fourth grade and her dad only went to the second grade. And she wasn't sure if they completed those years.

At any rate, neither of them went beyond the fourth grade of elementary school. My maternal grandfather Crit Wicker's dad died while he was a boy. He worked to support his younger sisters. Mom said he began working in the mines as a teenager. He didn't like that, and he got a job with the C&O Railroad. Mom didn't know how many years he worked there, but said he got a 40-year pin, so he worked there over 40 years.

My maternal grandmother Annie Hunter-Wicker was a housewife who bore eight children. She did home canning, used a washboard and a wringer washer to wash clothes, cooked from scratch, etc.

Crit and Annie grew a huge garden. They used well water, had an outhouse for a toilet, raised chickens, had a cow, etc. And when my mom got ill as a girl and needed more milk, they bought a second cow.

When they wanted natural gas in the hollow they lived in, mom reports that my grandfather strung the gas line himself from a neighbor's house I guess about ½ mile away. Then the gas company checked it out and made the connection to make it active.

I remember their involvement in an Old Regular Baptist Church that used no instrumental music.

I asked mom what her parents were like, and mom

said "they was good." She said her dad [I called him papaw.] was good to them, provided for them, told them stories, popped popcorn in summer and winter. She said he got up early and cooked breakfast, then he woke my grandmother [I called her mamaw.] up to eat with him since he didn't want to eat by himself. Mom said papaw usually left for work before the kids got up.

Mamaw would serve them leftovers and fixed more biscuits. Mom said they had biscuits and gravy and homemade syrup almost every day, along with some type of meat, sometimes cooked apples, etc. Mom said she "got along well with them." Mom said if her cover came off of her as a girl in the night, she got her dad to put it on instead of her mom. She said her mom "always had a baby in bed with her."

Mom said mamaw told her that papaw got baptized when she was a baby about nine months old. Mamaw dressed mom up nice to go to the baptism.

Mom said she remembered when her mother got baptized. Mamaw was baptized when she was in the eighth grade or a freshman in high school. During mom's younger years, mamaw was babysitting. The Old Regular Baptists did not have a Sunday School. Mom said she babysat the younger children while mamaw went to church.

Mom said she had a "happy childhood." In high school she said she'd go up to Cincinnati and stay a week or two with someone she knew (Evie was the person's name). Mom remembers that they rode, she guessed a trolley, into downtown Cincinnati to see a movie.

My Grandparents (Dad's Side of the Family)

My paternal grandparents both attended college. My paternal grandfather Edwin Joseph Gibson studied engineering at Washington & Lee before dropping out after his dad died to help support the family. But he developed a successful career as a land surveyor and mining engineer. He spent much time underground surveying mines.

My paternal grandmother Irene Depew-Gibson was an elementary school teacher at McVeigh in Pike County, Kentucky before marrying my grandfather. And she taught music lessons after they were married. She was probably one of the first college educated women in southeastern Kentucky.

They moved around a lot during my dad's childhood, before finally settling in Garrett. Before Garrett they lived in several towns in the coal mining areas of southeastern Kentucky, southwestern Virginia, and West Virginia.

Maternal and Paternal Grandparents As Neighbors

My maternal grandparents moved into a house at the head of a hollow (We pronounce it "holler" in southeastern Kentucky.) in Garrett in Floyd County, Kentucky when my mom was in elementary school.

My paternal grandparents moved into a house in what is called Baptist Bottom in Garrett when my dad was in high school. Baptist Bottom was at the foot of the hollow my mom's family lived in.

My paternal grandparents' house was located across the street from the Old Regular Baptist Church that my maternal grandparents attended.

Later my paternal grandparents and maternal

grandparents both moved into houses closer to downtown Garrett.

My Parents' Childhoods

Mom lived most of her childhood in the hollow in Garrett, Kentucky that they moved to when she was in grade school, perhaps the third or fourth grade. As I stated earlier, dad's family moved around much. After his dad and mom moved from Wayland in Floyd County to Baptist Bottom in Garrett while dad was in high school, dad continued going to Wayland High School, since he didn't want to change schools.

Dad said there were few cars then, but most drivers knew him and he typically caught a ride to school with someone. However, as dad told it, he was a fast runner and could make the trip on foot quickly. It was a few miles from Garrett to Wayland.

I asked mom how she and dad met. Mom says she thinks she was a sophomore or junior in high school when dad's family moved to Baptist Bottom in Garrett. She said she was friends with dad's younger sister, Sara, who was in mom's class. Mom told me that she [mom], her brother Rondal, Clarence Sexton, and Galen Sexton were all friends.

They would go to Sara's house. Sara's mom was in the hospital [probably due to her Parkinson's Disease]. Sara's brother Bill [my dad] was in college. I asked who cooked since Sara's mom was in the hospital, and she said she guessed Sara cooked, because she thinks dad's older sister Alice was already married at that time.

At some point dad and mom began dating, then got married on December 15th, 1954 while dad was still in college.

After they were married, while dad was still in college, mom said she babysat the two children of my dad's sister Alice [I called her Auntie Alice.] and her husband while my Auntie Alice was in the hospital with Dave, her youngest child. Mom said after she and dad got married in December 1954, since dad was still in college, she was staying with her mom and dad in the holler (hollow) in Garrett. My Auntie Alice's family also lived in Garrett.

My dad's mom suffered from Parkinson's Disease during her later years. My grandfather Gibson paid much for nurses and others to care for her 24/7. And I'm guessing he footed the bill for her travels to specialists in another state for treatment.

Her funeral when I was five years old is one of my earliest memories. My other three grandparents lived reasonably long lives, though all passed on many years ago.

My Autobiography

My autobiography (this book) is really only an incomplete rough draft. This is true in the sense that it omits many things and in the sense that my life and my search for the correct path is an ongoing search.

I omit some things due to limited space, as is the case in any autobiography or memoir. But some are omitted to spare others (and myself!) embarrassment, though I include at least a few embarrassing incidents. Despite the omissions, I sought to be completely truthful in what I wrote, in the sense of Ephesians 4:15, seeking to be truthful in a loving way. I'm far from perfect, but I feel much progress has been made toward the correct path through the grace and guidance of God, the highest righteous power, and others.

I sought in this book to focus on things that progressed me further along the path toward finding God's will for my life though I included some others too.

We moved several times during my childhood, although we always lived in southeastern Kentucky. This gave me exposure to different schools and enabled me to develop a variety of friends.

I've lived in Kentucky all my life, so I can't write how it compares to living in other places. But in southeastern Kentucky where I grew up from my birth in 1958 till my leaving for college in 1976, people seemed friendlier than what I read about people being like in some other areas.

Folks are friendly, helpful, nice. As you drove or walked by a house on a rural southeastern Kentucky road when I was growing up, often persons sitting on their front porches would wave at you, even if you were a stranger passing through. At least that's the way I remembered it being when I grew up there.

I like the independence of many hillbillies. In a sense hillbillies are mavericks. I am happy to consider myself a maverick in the good sense of the term. I hope to be a maverick led by the Holy Spirit.

My Books

My view is that this book is less important than my first two books. But readers may disagree.

In my first book, *True Christianity: It May Not Be What You Think*, I feel the Holy Spirit led me to offer some insights into what authentic Christianity is. Its third edition remains available for purchase from Amazon and bookstores.

In my second book, *Several True (I Think) Stories: Can Truth Be Stranger Than Fiction?*, I shared information about numerous unusual events, most of which I personally experienced or witnessed. Its second edition remains available for purchase from Amazon and bookstores.

This third book, *A Hillbilly: His Search for the Correct Path*, is designed to be more personal, to tell a story, the story of how I've progressed during my life toward fulfilling a dream since my childhood of being a writer. In a sense it is more like what I originally intended my first book to be like than either my first or second book.

I do want to repeat that it is only my personal story, not the story of all persons or all hillbillies.

My Early Childhood

Mom said she liked the name James, so that became my name. She stated dad asked how about Edwin for the middle name after his dad, and she agreed.

She told me she always wanted to call me James, not Jim, and thinks Bill Daniels (our next door neighbor in Jenkins where we moved when I was in high school) was the only one to ever call me Jim. I don't remember him doing it, but he may have. I also had some people call me Jim in Lexington and Nicholasville, after I moved away from Jenkins. But I stick to James now as I have most of my life.

When I asked what I was like as a baby, mom said

I had colic the first week I was home from the hospital. Mamaw, mom's mom Annie Hunter-Wicker, came over and stayed with her. My dad went over and got her after mom got out of the hospital. I cried and mamaw said I had the colic. The doctor gave me some medicine for it.

Mom said when she was pregnant with my sister Barbara that she phoned an African-American woman named Mary who had been a cook at the Benham Hotel, but had retired and was living in Cumberland (also in Harlan County) about coming to baby-sit me while she had Barbara, my younger sister.

Mom stated that dad told her it would be hard on me if Mary came in as a stranger. So mom said Mary came over once a week to do cleaning and to get to know me and played with me for 2 or 3 months before mom had my sister Barbara.

When mom was in the hospital giving birth to Barbara for perhaps 3 days including time after the birth, Mary babysat me. Mom informed that I would have Mary get down on the floor and ride her like a horsey. Mom said she told Mary she should have spanked me. Mom said Mary said "No, I couldn't do that. He would have cried for you and that would have broken my heart." I think mom said Mary stayed a week or two during days after she got out of the hospital. Her husband brought her in the morning and picked her up in the evening.

Mom said when I was little, I liked to bite people. She said when the family was visiting my maternal grandparents when I was perhaps a year old I crawled out to where mamaw (my grandmother) was drawing water from the well with a baler and pulled myself up by her dress tail and bit her. Mom said I wouldn't let go and she had to pull me off of mamaw.

Mom informed me that it was while I was a young boy that mamaw and papaw had a bathroom put in their house and an electric pump for the well. Their outhouse remained there though. Mom said even after they got a bathroom, papaw preferred using an outhouse when he could.

Our family moved from an apartment in Lynch, Kentucky to a house (actually a duplex mom said) a few doors away probably when my sister Barbara was less than one year old, mom said, so I would have been less than four years old. Mom stated that the house was a bit closer to the Tot Lot that I enjoyed playing at.

One of my earliest memories is of the day that my sister Barbara and I locked ourselves in the bathroom and didn't know how to unlock the door. Barb was scared.

Mom told me that I was probably about four years old when this happened and Barbara was probably about one-year-old. Mom said she had already phoned dad at work and he was going to get someone with a ladder to try to get the window open. But mom managed to give me instructions to tell me how to unlock the door. Mom said I never did that again or if I did I knew how to unlock it.

I don't remember it personally, but mom told me that on another occasion I used a broom to unlatch the screen door to go out to play in the yard, since I was too short to reach the latch. Barbara got out and crossed the street and went up the road. A neighbor phoned mom and asked "Have you lost something? We've got a little baby up here walking around." Mom said she talked to me, and I never did that again.

Mom said I also used to sneak out and go to the Tot Lot, a children's play area a few doors down from where we lived. Dad and mom both told me about a time I pushed a friend off a wall at the Tot Lot that resulted in a broken bone for him. Mom said he had a broken ankle. I don't remember it. She told me that she thought I was five years old, and it happened during the summer shortly before we moved away.

She said the guy I pushed was about 6 months younger than me, perhaps 4 ½ year old. She informed me that he was dad's boss's son. Their family lived next to the Tot Lot. Mom told me that they had 11 or 12 children, and a bunch of us were playing.

Mom said she phoned them and apologized profusely, but the woman stated that we were just boys playing where we shouldn't, and he could have just as easily pushed me off.

I remember for some reason enjoying sneaking off behind a bush or tree to poop instead of using the bathroom when we lived at Lynch. Somehow I got happiness out of it. Maybe I experienced the type of pleasure my papaw did from his outhouse.

Mom and dad said I went to the Methodist Church while we lived at Lynch. Mom said dad's boss was Catholic and took some of his kids to the Catholic Church, and his wife was a Methodist and took at least one of them to the Methodist Church. Dad said a friend of mine went there, and I wanted to go with him.

According to mom, I went to church with a woman

who lived between the apartment building we had lived in and the duplex we moved to later. Then the woman stayed for church and mom either came and got me or I walked home. Mom said that I told her "I can walk home by myself" so she let me sometimes when it was pretty weather.

She said I walked from the church to the sidewalk across the street from our house by myself. She said she knew about what time church let out and could see me walking most of the way and she thinks there were some steps that led down to the sidewalk near our house at that time. She then walked across the road with me.

When mom, a sister, a niece, and I visited Lynch in 2019, I was surprised at how far the Methodist Church (in the same building as when we lived in Lynch) was from where we had lived. It was a fairly long walk for a preschooler.

Mom also said she and dad went to a movie theater in Cumberland some before I was born when they were living at the Benham Hotel. She said they also went fishing some in the river and in a lake.

After I was born, when they went fishing, mom said that dad stated you couldn't catch any fish with James around. He said I scared the fish away throwing rocks in the water, but she said dad said it nicely, knowing I was a young boy, and he wasn't upset about it.

As a young boy, I remember picking something dirty up from the ground such as a coin and eating with dirty hands. I didn't think about it until mom told me not to do it. Then, she added that I didn't need to worry about it, she did.

Did she say that just to keep me from worrying about it, or do mothers have some type of "magic" to protect children from catching diseases after eating with dirty hands? I don't know.

I remember being asked to pick the color of the family's new car in 1962, and choosing blue, and being surprised that it was a lighter blue than I'd expected.

My paternal grandmother passed on when I was five years old, and we attended her funeral, as I mentioned earlier. I described part of that experience in my first two books and how I felt she moved in the casket and was alive. You might say I made a scene.

One Christmas when I was young, we stayed overnight at mamaw and papaw's house (Crit and Annie Wickers') at Garrett in Floyd County. I was concerned Santa Claus wouldn't know where we were and wouldn't leave any gifts. Mom said I asked "Will Santa find us?" She assured me he would.

I was also concerned that due to mamaw and papaw having a fire in their fireplace Santa wouldn't be able to get down the chimney or would be burned. I considered getting some water to put the fire out. Mamaw made it clear that wasn't going to happen. She stated "You're not going to put my fire out. I'll freeze to death. Santa Claus can come in the door like everyone else, if he comes."

Mom stated to me that she told me Santa had a fireproof suit. And I think my papaw said he'd leave the door unlocked for Santa.

Mom told me years later that she, dad, her sister Lavone, and she thinks her sister Renessa had a lot of fun carrying gifts up the hollow, which our car didn't go up due to a snowfall. Mom said she told me Santa might have left some stuff at our house that was big. She said that was the year I got a pegboard that had a blackboard on one side which was left at our home in Harlan County.

Mom said I colored on a post on mamaw's porch when I was a little boy, perhaps 3 or 4. As I remember that incident, I was a bit older than 3 or 4, and I didn't actually do it, but mamaw thought I did and accused me by mistake.

At any rate, mamaw had trouble getting it off, and I told her something like "whoever put that on there probably didn't want it to come off." She became angry and chased after me with a broom or mop, but didn't catch me. It's the only time I remember her being angry with me. I'm not sure what she would have done if she'd caught me. But I'm glad I didn't have to find out.

When I was five years old we moved from Lynch to Stone in Pike County, Kentucky.

Chapter 2: Growing Up, Early Grade School Years

Our family (mom, dad, my younger sister Barbara, and I) moved to Stone, Kentucky when I was five years old. Mom said it was during the summer, warm weather, and the grass was high in the yard of the house we moved into. Dad had already been working at Stone and staying at the Club House (a company-owned building for guests, activities, etc.). He would drive back to Lynch on Friday evening, mom thought, and back to Stone early Monday morning for work.

Interestingly, my paternal grandmother Irene Depew-Gibson had lived in the Stone Clubhouse while she taught school at McVeigh according to my dad, who said that was probably before she married his dad.

During this time when dad was commuting back and forth before the entire family moved to Stone, dad had a bleeding ulcer and almost died. My guess is that the stresses of the new job, long hours of travel and work, etc., were a factor. Dad received blood transfusions, recovered, and I am thankful lived until the age of 82, passing on to heaven on April 27th, 2013.

President John F. Kennedy Assassination and Funeral

The assassination of President John F. Kennedy occurred November 22, 1963 while we lived at Stone. I was five years old. I remember watching television news coverage afterward. I saw the President's son, who was probably about my age, standing respectfully at attention during I guess the President's funeral procession.

I remember thinking how well he behaved and how his mom must have instructed him carefully on how to behave, just as my mom instructed me carefully on our way to my grandmother's funeral. He seemed to follow instructions better than me.

I remember one day, which I guess was the day of the President's funeral, that I wanted to go outside to play and mom said to stay in since it looked like it was going to rain, and she didn't want me to get dirty, because we were getting ready to leave I think to visit my grandparents.

She suggested I watch cartoons on television. I turned the TV on. It was only showing coverage of I guess the funeral and/or funeral procession for President Kennedy. I think it was the funeral procession that I referenced in a previous paragraph.

I watched a replay of the assassination on multiple occasions. The replay showed the President in a convertible in his motorcade.

In southeastern Kentucky where we lived, there were few convertibles partially due to their cost and perhaps even more so due to the risk of a lump of coal hitting the car from an overloaded coal truck driving down the road without a cover on it. At any rate, my thought was, I figured the President had a lot of money, and I wondered why the President couldn't afford a car with a roof on it.

A Visit To My Maternal Grandparents' and Prayer

On a visit to my maternal grandparents' house, when I was a young boy, I was curious how much water was in a large water barrel they had under a downspout for the house. They used the barrel to catch rainwater coming off the roof.

I determined to find out. I turned it over. Mom was upset with me. Mom said mamaw might need that water if her well ran dry. But mamaw was nice about it.

I asked mamaw something like "How often does the well run dry?" She replied something like "The well doesn't run dry. If it's getting low, I pray for rain. And I don't wait for the well to go dry to pray for rain."

Preparing for School

I remember looking forward to starting the first grade. I remember going to the Stone Grade School for something, perhaps preregistration. I thought it was time for school. I wanted to stay for school. Mom said it wasn't time yet.

A Babysitter

Mom was a stay at home mom. My parents seldom left me with a babysitter. But I clearly remember one occasion when they did. I remember a girl who lived next door to us at Stone babysitting me, and me threatening to break a window for some reason, and then hitting it, not intending to hit it hard enough to break it. But I did.

The babysitter was scared and wanted me to go with her next door to her mom, but I didn't want to. After checking me to verify I was okay, she told me to stay right there and not move, and she was going to go get her mother next door. I did. She did.

She and her mom quickly came over. Her mom checked me out, verifying I was okay. My mom said the girl was a teenager, and she thought her first name was Barbara. Mom said dad wanted to go to an auction and wanted mom to go with him. Mom didn't want to go, but dad wanted her to and said they could get a babysitter.

On another occasion, I remember being out in our yard, and the same girl who babysat me was in her yard with her mom. I threw something playfully at her.

She responded by throwing something at me. I think it was a metal protractor or triangle. When she saw it was going to hit me, she screamed for me to duck, but I turned around and it hit me just above my eye. She was remorseful and felt terrible about it. It bled, but as I recall no lasting damage was done.

School at Stone

I remember my first grade teacher at Stone Grade School (Mrs. Conley?) talking about our reading book, which I think was titled *The Little White House*. She said she liked the book and felt it was a nice reading book, but would have liked it to have the word "home" in the title instead of "house."

She asked if any of us knew the difference between a house and a home. I raised my hand high, confident I knew the answer and wanting her to call on me. She (I read her thoughts I think) thought "he never raises his hand for anything, I won't embarrass him by picking him, since he doesn't know the answer."

She looked around the room. And she continued speaking, stating that the pages on the inside of the book made it clear that it was a home instead of just a house. I looked wistfully at the pages inside the book as my teacher continued talking, then suddenly the teacher stopped talking. No one else seemed to speak, so it was quiet.

Surprised, I turned around, looked up, and saw the teacher staring at me. I was embarrassed. I read her thoughts again I think; she was thinking, "He does know the difference. I never would have thought it."

I was blessed with a wonderful family, but I felt that the family in the home in my reading book was even better, one without any arguments between parents, living together in harmony always.

On another occasion in the first grade at Stone, the teacher asked us to stack our reading books. I wanted to see how tall the stack would be, so I waited near the end of the line, watching the stack get taller. I wondered how high it would get, and if it would topple over. Then after observing the stack getting high, I ran or walked so fast over to put mine up that I almost knocked some girl down, I think.

Instead of reprimanding me, my teacher nicely said something about it being nice of me to wait and let others go first, though softly adding that I got a bit too fast at the end and almost knocked someone down.

On another occasion in the first grade at Stone, noticing that I did not drink my milk, my teacher asked me to verify I wasn't allergic to it, then asked me to drink it before leaving the lunchroom. I did.

But, she didn't seem to notice I had drunk it, and I didn't want to walk over to where she was to show her I had drunk it, for some reason, perhaps my shyness. And I didn't want to leave the lunchroom without permission.

So, I hit my milk container down hard on the table to get her attention. She didn't seem to notice. So, I did it at least one or two other times until she noticed. Another teacher beside her said I was making a scene. But, my teacher nicely stated that I was just letting her know I had finished my milk as she had asked. She told that teacher that she had forgotten about it. My teacher then told me that since I had drunk all my milk, I could leave the lunchroom. I appreciated her tact and understanding.

On another occasion in the first grade, we were playing "King of the Hill" on a small hill in the schoolyard during recess. I wanted to be the "king of the hill," so I went up and pushed one or more others off. We got in trouble, and a spanking. The teacher felt one or more of us could have been injured. That's the only spanking I remember in first grade, and one of only two or three I recall at school during all my school years. But maybe there were a few that I forgot.

We had a fireplace in our house at Stone. Mom said I threw a firecracker in it, even though I wasn't supposed to have a firecracker. Thankfully I wasn't injured, though I think it scared mom.

We moved from Stone while I was still in the first grade.

Living in Maytown/Langley in Floyd County, Kentucky

During the middle of my first grade school year, our family moved from Stone to Langley, also known as Maytown, in Floyd County, Kentucky.

I remember the house we rented at Maytown had a gas furnace. When we were shown the house before moving in, the man showing it to us told us it had a gas furnace. He pointed out the pilot light deep below the floor and talked about lighting it. Dad was concerned about the danger, stating he'd never had a gas furnace before. Mom said she knew about gas. Dad told the man and mom that she'd take care of the pilot light. I was a bit worried, but mom eased my worries.

When we first moved to Maytown, mom met me at school and walked home with me. One day we got out of school early, so mom wasn't there yet to pick me up.

I waited, thinking about what to do. I didn't want to talk to the teacher about it due I think to my shyness. Yet, I knew I wasn't supposed to walk home by myself.

After a while, the teacher told me I could go home. As I was leaving, as an afterthought, she said to another teacher beside her, something like "I think his mom normally picks him up. I wonder if I did the right thing. Well, he's gone now."

I walked to the road, and looked carefully to make sure it was clear in each direction. I was confident I could cross safely. But I wanted someone to see me doing so, so I'd have a witness that I'd done so safely. I waited, but no one came by.

Then the postmaster came out from the post office across the street. I didn't want him to help me across the street. I wanted to demonstrate I could cross safely alone. So, I started to cross. He said wait, but I wanted to cross alone to prove I could do it, so I looked again carefully, then ran quickly across before he could cross the street.

When I got to our rented house, I convinced mom I had walked home safely. She then let me walk home alone daily after that.

From early childhood I loved to read. While we lived at Maytown, dad and mom ordered me a subscription to Dr. Seuss books since I enjoyed them so much.

Staying Up All Night and a Long Trip

I remember staying up all night on a drive with dad, my paternal grandfather Edwin Joseph Gibson, my Uncle Jennings Martin, and another relative to visit my dad's uncle Guy Gibson and his wife Hazel. I wanted to stay awake all night to prove I could do it. Dad drove. He and I talked much during the night as I recall. And I think I succeeded in staying awake all night.

The trip took place, as I recall, while we lived at Maytown, possibly the summer after I was in the first grade, at age 7. But mom said it happened when we lived at Lynch during the summer when I was about five, before I started school.

In addition to visiting Guy and Hazel on the trip, we also visited a navy shipyard, which I think was in nearby Norfolk.

Dad had told me that during the trip we would see the ocean, a huge amount of water so large that it would be water as far as I could see. At some point during the trip as we were driving in eastern Virginia, we drove across a long bridge, actually a combination of one or more bridges and one or more tunnels that was miles long all together.

I could only see water all around us at some points. I thought we were crossing the ocean.

In my second book *Several True (I Think) Stories*, I discuss an unusual conversation I overheard that my dad and my grandfather had with Guy during the trip.

From Maytown we moved to Lackey.

Lackey

We moved to Lackey, also in Floyd County, a few miles from Maytown perhaps the summer after I completed the first grade or when I was in the early part of the second grade. I think mom told me once that dad drove me to school at Garrett on his way to work at the beginning of my second grade school year, so I wouldn't have to change schools during the year. Though Lackey had a school, I went to Garrett perhaps a mile from Lackey. My mom went to school at Garrett most of her childhood, from about the third or fourth grade through her high school graduation.

While living at Lackey, I began reading some Bobbsey Twins books that I think dad had bought at an auction in a box that contained many other books. I loved them. I soon began reading other mystery series like Nancy Drew and The Hardy Boys.

I seemed to do well in school overall. I remember my second grade teacher at Garrett complimenting me on my use of phonetics versus the look-say method of pronouncing words that apparently was taught there.

I also remember my second grade teacher selecting me when an upper level class teacher asked for a second grader to solve arithmetic problems. This upper level teacher apparently had told his class that a second grader could solve some problems that several in his class had difficulty with. I solved I think two out of three of them. My cousin Dave Martin was one of the students in the upper level class, and he seemed proud of me. I'm not sure if he was one of the students who had experienced difficulty with the problems.

Mom and dad taught me at an early age the importance of studying to do well in school. And though we did not attend church for most of my childhood, they also taught me the importance of being truthful and honest. I learned basic morals from them.

While I always did and still do fall far short of perfection, I am seeking to progress closer toward it. I know that only through the grace and guidance of God can I succeed in continuing to progress that way.

While in the second grade at Garrett, I remember being attracted to a particular girl and wanting to kiss her on the cheek. I moved my chair a bit closer, and kept gradually moving it closer. Fortunately, my teacher came up and made me stop before I got close enough.

I loved the 1960s Batman television show as a child. In addition to the television show, I enjoyed the Batman trading cards I had collected, as well as a Batman & Robin Society Charter Member button, and a Batman ring. I also had a Batman t-shirt.

But I realized that there was far too much Batman memorabilia being sold. Once when mom asked me at a checkout counter of a store if I wanted a particular Batman item there, knowing how much I loved the Batman show and items related to it that I owned, I said no. And I wasn't interested in that particular item, whatever it was.

On another occasion, I remember one of my second grade classmates and I were walking on the school grounds discussing how excessive the Batman merchandising was. We thought it was ridiculous even as second graders. We did enjoy the television show though.

While we lived at Lackey, I remember one night being awake a long time, fearful of dying for some reason. Mom apparently heard me crying and came in asking what was wrong and sought to comfort me. I don't know what led to that fear of dying. I only remember that one occasion, but mom in a recent phone conversation stated I expressed those feelings multiple times as a young child.

On another occasion while we lived on Lackey Hill, I found what I thought might be a snake, and told mom who was nearby talking to our neighbor. I wanted her to come look.

But instead she said to get a stick to poke it, a long stick. I went to do so. I looked to where I thought the snake was, then I reached down to pick up a nearby stick. The stick moved. It apparently was a black racer snake. I told mom the thing I thought was a snake wasn't one but the stick I started to pick up was. Fortunately the snake ran away fast in the opposite direction from the one I went.

On another occasion when we lived on Lackey Hill, dad was on a ladder next to the house and asked me to climb up and hand him something. Mom told me no, not to do it. She said it was too dangerous.

I think she told dad that I might fall and be hurt badly or killed. Dad said it wasn't that dangerous.

I obeyed mom, even though I thought I could safely climb up the ladder and hand dad whatever it was he wanted.

I think the neighbor mom was talking to at the time felt mom was wrong, and that I should have obeyed my dad, saying even if an accident occurred it might be God's will, some kids don't have a chance, if I was reading her thoughts correctly.

Often, it seems I can read the thoughts of others—of course often others can read my thoughts too or seem to. At any rate, I felt I was blessed immeasurably and not a person without a chance.

While we lived at Lackey, dad bought me a football, football helmet, shoulder pads, etc. I only remember playing with dad with them once. Mom felt dad was being too rough, and I'd be hurt. My safety equipment was too big for me, and I think dad was a bit rough. As I recall, that was the last time I played football, for better or worse.

In the Bobbsey Twins books I read while on Lackey Hill, they had a tree house. I felt it would fun if I had one. So I got some boards from over the hill that I assumed were garbage. I began nailing them onto a tree limb. When mom saw me doing it, she said I was doing it the wrong way and would kill the tree. I think I asked her what was the right way, and she said she didn't know. She said to build the house in the wood pile over the hill. I started doing so.

When dad came in from work, he walked over to where I was doing it, and stating I was doing it the wrong way and it wouldn't hold together. I said it would when I finished.

He suggested that instead of the house that he build a wooden chair with a compartment underneath it for my toys. I said a wooden chair probably wouldn't be comfortable to sit in. Then dad added, a wooden compartment under the chair wouldn't be big enough for all my toys, maybe a box would be better.

So, dad built two large boxes, one for me and one for my sister Barbara, and painted them green. Though they were boxes, not a tree house, they were large enough to play in at times when they weren't filled with stuff.

Also while we lived on Lackey Hill, I asked dad for a sandbox. I thought one would be fun. I think he'd just gotten in from a tiring day at work. When I asked, he said build it yourself. I said I didn't have any sand. He said make some, crush some sandstone rocks.

I did. And I told my younger sister Barbara that if she wanted to play in it, she had to help me. She did. We worked on it quite a while. I was proud of our efforts.

And at least once, I asked mom for some vinegar to test some rocks to see if they were sandstone or limestone before crushing them. Dad on some earlier occasion had told/showed me how to use vinegar (which creates a visible reaction on limestone) to test whether a rock was limestone or sandstone.

After my sister and I had worked on it for what seemed like a long time, hours or days, I'm not sure, dad came over and said he'd get some sand for me.

At that point, proud of my work, I wanted to finish it myself, but he said he'd get some real sand, which would be much better. Some of my sand wasn't crushed completely. My sister Barbara strongly agreed with him. And dad hauled some sand from somewhere for our sandbox.

During one winter, after snow covered the paved road leading up to our house on Lackey Hill, I wanted to ride my sled off all the way to the bottom. Mom told me not to, a car might come up. Normally few cars came up the hill, so I told her that was unlikely, though after she said it, I thought of dad coming up early from work or someone else coming up. I asked mom to watch for cars. She said she had work to do. And she went back inside.

I decided to give it a try. My sister Barbara wanted to too. I said I'd go first. She said no, she wanted to go first. I was afraid she'd be hurt, if not by a car coming up the hill, then by a wreck or running into something at a high speed at the bottom of the hill. I was concerned about it myself. And I thought I might try to stop partway down the hill.

I felt it was too dangerous for her to try first, and she was adamant that I not go first. Finally, I suggested that we would ride down together. She agreed.

I got on the sled, and she got on top. I told her to hold on tight. She did.

We rode down, but I was afraid we'd get up too much speed and hit something at the bottom of the hill or something might come up, and I couldn't see too well with her on top of me.

So I steered to the side of the road to stop. As I did, I repeated to my sister to hold on tight. She did.

Unfortunately, there was a barbed wire fence there that I didn't see initially. It hit Barb. She said I hit it on purpose and was going to tell mom. I don't remember what mom said or did.

The house we rented on Lackey Hill had a cistern, a cement-lined pond. It connected via a pipe to a house roof drainage pipe to catch rainwater runoff.

Dad enjoyed fishing. On one occasion when dad and I went fishing, dad suggested bringing back the fish we caught to put in the pond.

We did. I carried them on a stringer from the lake or pond where we were fishing back to our vehicle. I was concerned they might not live till we got back to our vehicle. But dad said they would.

I dipped them into mud puddles along the way to try to give them a bit of water to help them stay alive, then put them in a bucket with water we had at the vehicle. Some of them died, which I hated. But others lived.

We then drove back to our house with them and placed them in the cistern.

We still had fish living in our cement pond/cistern when we were preparing to move away from Lackey to Glo. Mom stated the new residents might fill in the pond and suggested dad and I take the fish to the creek. Dad and I did. I enjoyed watching them swim away.

Glo

We moved from Lackey to Glo. Glo was very close to Wayland. Wayland is where my dad went to high school. I started the third grade there.

The Wayland School was near our house, actually within sight of it I think. I enjoyed the independence of being able to walk to school.

Dad told me he had walked to Wayland School some and said there used to be a railroad tie beside the railroad tracks that led across a small ditch below the hillside leading up to the school.

I felt proud to be walking in dad's steps in a sense.

I wondered if the railroad tie I walked across was the same one dad had walked across many years earlier.

While we lived at Glo, mom tried unsuccessfully to teach me to tie my shoes. She apparently waited until nearly time for dad to come in from work one day to try. She may have tried teaching me before this occasion, but I only remember this one particular occasion.

She had not succeeded by the time dad got in from work. She asked dad to try.

He succeeded in teaching me to tie them with one bow. He was probably tired after a long day's work, but he patiently tried teaching me to tie them with two bows too. I failed. Then he provided more guidance and asked me to try again. I failed again. He asked me to try harder. I still failed. Then he asked me to try my best. After I tried again and failed, I said I tried my best.

Then frustrated, he said "Your best ain't worth s_ _ _. He was probably very tired after a long day of work, more tired from trying to teach me, and probably hungry too. And as I stated earlier, I think mom had been teaching me instead of preparing supper.

I could tell from the expression on dad's face that he regretted what he said immediately after he said it. Then he said softly to mom, something like, "James is tired now and I'm tired too. We'll try it again some time later." As far as I remember, we never did. I frequently wore slip-on shoes.

Some years later during the summer before my freshman year in high school, I decided to teach myself how to tie shoes with two bows. I knew that the next school year in PE class I'd be wearing lace-up gym shoes and would be embarrassed if I couldn't tie them myself.

The shoes I wore that summer were slip-ons. But one day during that summer when I was home alone, I decided to devote an hour or a few hours to practicing tying shoes. I got a pair of dad's shoes and practiced tying them.

I was pleasantly surprised that I succeeded in learning how after only minutes. It was much easier than I'd expected. I may still not tie shoes the way typical people do, but my two-bow method does work and seems similar to the "correct" way.

I'm not sure when I began writing stories for fun. But either it was while I was in the third grade at Glo or earlier that I began writing very short, simple stories. They were poorly written. I know because some years later while I was still in elementary school, I threw them away, embarrassed at their poor quality.

But at least one of my relatives, my aunt Lavone, complimented me on my poorly written stories and expressed enjoyment at reading them. I think she was being kind and using hyperbole.

I'm not sure if the stories were good even by third grade standards. But I appreciated her compliments.

In some ways Lavone was like an older sister to me. She was eight years old when I was born. She still lived with my grandparents during much of my childhood. She often visited us, as well as us visiting them.

I remember one day at recess in the 3rd grade at Wayland being embarrassed that I didn't know how to play ball (either baseball or softball I think) and standing with a few other people instead of trying to play or telling them I didn't know how.

I also remember one day in the school library wanting to read a long book in the school library like a Hardy Boys mystery and a library staff member suggested I read a shorter one like Dr. Seuss that was at an easier reading level. Someone (I think my teacher) said I was a good reader and could read the longer book. But, I think she agreed with the staff member that for the time in the library a shorter book would be more appropriate.

The urinals in the boys' restroom that my class used at Wayland Grade School were very long. One day some of us boys had a peeing contest to see who could pee the furthest distance. I peed so far that I peed beyond the urinal into the floor. I think I won the contest. But I and some others got paddled. I deserved it. Some janitor had to clean pee out of the floor after I'd peed longer than the urinal. At a Wayland School reunion for all students who had attended the school that my family attended, long after I was an adult, I toured part of the school. I looked again at the long urinal I'd peed into. It was fairly long. I must have peed big.

I remember at least one trip walking from Glo to mamaw and papaw's (Crit and Annie Wickers') house in Garrett with my mom and my sister Barbara when we lived at Glo. It was only a few miles. I enjoyed taking that walk along the railroad tracks and talking with mom and my sister as we walked.

I especially enjoyed crossing one or two trestles, though I was concerned about a train possibly coming.

Mom said if we were ever caught in the middle of the trestle and couldn't get off before the train came, there was usually a platform in the middle. But the platforms were typically small and might vibrate much when a train was passing. She urged us to try to listen for a train and watch for one before we got on the trestle. She mentioned getting down and listening at the rail, which would convey the sound of the train from farther away than we could see or hear while walking. Her dad who worked for the C&O Railroad had taught her that.

Now there are laws against walking on railroad tracks. Maybe there were then, but the railroad tracks then at least typically went in a straighter and more level direction than the roadways cars drove on. Furthermore, there were no sidewalks beside the roadways there.

We didn't live very long at Glo. We moved away from Glo when I was still in the third grade.

Chapter 3: Middle Elementary School Years at Stone

Living at Stone the Second Time

During the school year that I was in the third grade we moved from Glo back to Stone. We had lived at Stone earlier. This time we lived on the Clubhouse Lawn in a nicer house. Our house and others on the Clubhouse Lawn had radiator heat with steam generated from a coal-fired furnace in a building near the Clubhouse Lawn. We lived there probably a bit over four years, moving again in February 1971 when I was in the seventh grade.

Those four years or so were the years when I probably developed my somewhat unique hillbilly accent that I still retain. And I probably developed the most neighborhood childhood friends during that time.

Stone was a coal mining town that still had a company store. As I recall, the company store was the only store in town. We lived in a company house.

But mom and dad did most of their shopping at nearby Williamson, West Virginia (perhaps 8 miles away?) instead of the company store. Even if mom just needed a couple of items, such as milk and bread, she typically went to a grocery store in Huddy that was probably less than a mile from our house instead of shopping at the Stone company store. She and/or dad said company store prices were too high. Since our house was at the lower end of the camp, that grocery store in Huddy was probably almost as close as the company store to where we lived anyway.

I cherish many fond memories of Stone. I had lots of fun.

It was while we lived at Stone that I threw away the simplistic, childish stories I'd written some time before moving back to Stone. However, I did begin occasionally making journal entries in a journal I started while at Stone. I regret not doing so more regularly.

I loved to read. During my time at Stone, mom and dad bought me many books. I also checked many out of the Williamson, West Virginia Public Library. The Williamson Public Library offered checkout privileges to persons living in neighboring areas of Kentucky.

After Stone opened a small public library, I checked out some books there too. Dad played a leading role in establishing the Stone Public Library.

I rarely checked out books from the Runyon Elementary School Public Library. Even when required to check out a book from it, I often kept the same book from the Runyon Elementary School library and renewed it. However, sometimes during library period I would walk around the school's stacks and skim several books that appealed to me. I loved reading and learning.

I also enjoyed discussing various issues. During library period, a friend and I often enjoyed discussions on various topics. At the time I thought we had some nice insights, worthy or superior to many of the views expressed by adults. But they may have been silly. I remember little about those discussions now.

I also enjoyed offering logical support for my

views. My maternal great grandmother (my maternal grandmothers' mom, whom I called maw) said I'd make a good lawyer because I argued my point so well. I enjoyed supporting my view with logical points, and typically sought to be on the right side so logical points did support my view.

While we lived at Stone (I think it was this second time we lived there.), mom and dad decided to go to church. Dad wanted to go to the Methodist Church. Mom wanted to go to the Baptist Church. They agreed to let me decide.

We walked along up to a large brick building, and dad said something like "there's the Baptist Church and it looks like it's empty and down here is the Methodist Church and we began walking toward it. Then mom said something like "that's not the Baptist Church. The Baptist Church is over here, you need to let him see it and be fair." She pointed to a white wood frame building down a side street from the street we were on. Dad said she wins, and I think put his arms around my shoulder, and we turned and walked over to the Baptist Church.

The door was open and I could hear some loud speaking/preaching quite a distance away from it. Apparently we were late.

I fondly recall attending the Stone Baptist Church, and how my Sunday School teacher taught us about Jesus and how he loved all children. Then in church the pastor spoke about hellfire and damnation. Mom said he wasn't talking about me, he was talking about dad, though dad seemed nice to me.

Soon afterward I think dad and mom stopped

attending Sunday School and church. But I attended Sunday School only with neighbors for a while. I walked to and from Sunday School with a couple that lived perhaps 5-8 houses from us in the direction of the church. I discussed why I stopped attending there in my first book, *True Christianity: It May Not Be What You Think*, so I won't repeat it.

I remember one day mom and dad were helping me pick out a personal Bible at a 5 & 10 cent store in Williamson, West Virginia. Many if not most of my Sunday School classmates already had Bibles and I didn't.

Perhaps it's a bit surprising that dad and mom hadn't already bought me a Bible, considering how many other books I had. Mom and dad had purchased many books for me.

Mom wanted my personal Bible to be the King James Version. Dad preferred a simpler modern English version. Mom also wanted one with a concordance. The book mom picked out also had the words attributed to Jesus in red. A timeline in the back listed dates from the creation.

Dad wasn't happy about that timeline. But mom said they'd probably researched it and those dates were accurate. Dad said I didn't necessarily need to agree with those dates. That Bible mom liked best is the one that we ended up getting.

I still have it, although I now have several other Bibles of perhaps a dozen different versions too. If I remember correctly, it was either in January 1967 or January 1968, shortly before either my ninth or my tenth birthday that they bought it for me.

I was very shy. I remember a school play probably when I was in the third grade soon after we moved to Stone. In the play, I was to come from behind a box and say I think one short line.

When it came time for me to, I didn't. I don't remember if I had forgotten my line, or if I was just too shy to come out in front of a group of people to say it. Definitely the latter, and maybe both.

The play director (my teacher I think) coaxed me to come out, stating I didn't need to say my line, but to just come out so they could see me. I stayed where I was.

Then I heard my mom's voice. Apparently my mom came down the aisle toward the front, and said something like "You don't have to come out, James, if you don't want to." I think that embarrassed me even more.

I think I heard my teacher and someone else, possibly another teacher, talking to each other saying something like "His mother is the problem."

I'm sure mom had good intentions. Mom was a bit strict on me and a bit overprotective. In some ways that was a great thing. I avoided the problems many of my classmates experienced, and I'm grateful to mom (and dad) for that. But in other ways, it probably held me back in some social areas. However, I feel blessed to have the dad and mom I did. Their strengths as parents certainly outweighed their weaknesses. After all, there are no perfect parents, or perfect children.

I was introspective in some ways, often thinking. I remember one day as I was preparing to get a drink from a water fountain at Runyon, I wondered about the possibility of getting diseases from drinking after someone else from it. I remember deciding that if I only drank the water and my mouth didn't touch the metal spout that I would be okay, as long as I let it run a bit first.

I didn't realize it until one day in the fourth grade, but there were apparently some very poor persons living in the area. I remember one day when I was in the fourth grade, my teacher instructed one girl to put her shoes on. She said she didn't have any.

The teacher replied, something like "we'll see if we can do something about that." The girl replied defiantly something like "My family doesn't take handouts." At that time at least, apparently a lot of persons in southeastern Kentucky took pride in doing things for themselves, living within their means, and not taking outside help, even when in somewhat desperate circumstances.

I was blessed with some wonderful friends/playmates during my time at Stone. We would ride bicycles, hike the mountains, talk, and played a lot of games. We played croquet, Rook,® Monopoly,® Clue,® chess, checkers, Stratego,® Risk,® Battleship,® Chinese checkers, and others. Often mom would play, and sometimes dad would play.

My mom was relatively strict on me. She rarely let me go to friends' houses to play. But she welcomed them to come to our house to play games.

My weakest subject in elementary school was art. I was terrible at drawing. My art teacher graded leniently.

But my art weakness carried over a bit to other subjects. In the fourth grade, I got D's in writing four times. I got a bit better in the fifth grade at least temporarily, as I discuss later.

My dad enjoyed having his back scratched. And for some reason he had trouble scratching it. He would sometimes require me or my sister to scratch it, and sometimes paid us to do it. I wondered if that was common for all dads?

I remember one day that my fourth grade class had a spelling bee. I was a good speller and thought I had a chance to win. But I misspelled a word, felt bad about losing, and also thought about what a tough word it was.

I think I read the teacher's [Mrs. Eunice Runyon's] thoughts and her thinking was that I was a good speller, and she wasn't sure if anyone else could have spelled that particular word, but it's the one that came up for me, and that she'd make a note of it, and maybe my teacher next year would have time for more spelling bees.

I also remember one day Mrs. Runyon asked us to take some time to read in our science textbooks. I remember reading in it, and feeling it was more like an outdated second grade reading book than a science book, and that I learned more science from newspaper reading.

Again it seemed I read her thoughts, and she was thinking that none of the female teachers at Runyon were good at science (sorry for the sexist statement!) and it might be better if they didn't teach it. When I got into an upper grade she thought Mr. Buford Cool might do me very well in science with a much better book or maybe he didn't even use a book, but he did much more in-depth coverage of science. He did do more in-depth teaching, but I didn't do that well, as I discuss a bit later.

My fifth grade teacher and sixth grade homeroom teacher was Miss Mary Elizabeth Williamson. I think she never married. She made class fun. She was likely my favorite elementary school teacher. We seemed to have a spelling bee and an arithmetic match almost every week. I won the majority of the spelling bees and more arithmetic matches than anyone except Bud Williams. I was a competitive person who enjoyed winning contests, though I sought to play fairly.

As mentioned earlier, I was very shy. I remember one day when we had a spelling bee, before the weekly class spelling bee, Ms. Williamson said it would be a special one because the winner of this particular spelling bee would be our class's representative and in competition with the other 5th grade class(es) in the school to decide who would be going to Pikeville to participate in the Pike County spelling bee. She said she thought our class had an excellent chance, apparently due to my spelling skills. I remember being nervous about the possibility of being in the county spelling bee. I either misspelled a word deliberately or due in part to nervousness and lack of focus.

Apparently Ms. Williamson passed on her impression that I'd deliberately misspelled a word due to nervousness. One Saturday as my family was going to visit my grandparents, dad had us stop at Pikeville and we went into an auditorium. Dad said it was the day of the county spelling bee and he thought this was where it was being held, and the spelling bee might still be going on.

We watched it a few minutes. Then dad said something like "You could do that, couldn't you." And I felt that I could. This incident helped significantly as one step in overcoming my shyness.

I went on to participate in county spelling bees in the sixth, seventh, and eighth grades, as well as my freshman and sophomore years of high school. The school I attended my last 1 ½ years did not participate in the spelling bee, so I didn't participate my junior or senior year.

Ms. Williamson also occasionally read to us from an entertaining book of some type. After we finished our work, she would also let us read in some of the books she had in the classroom. I sometimes hurried to finish my work to do so.

When my handwriting was poor on certain things, she had me write it over again neater. She improved my handwriting significantly at least temporarily. But I still struggle with handwriting.

My thoughts seem to come to me faster than I can write them, so I start writing faster and faster to get them down before I forget them, and my writing is sloppy. Poor motor skills may be a bit of a factor too.

Ms. Williamson also allotted some time for singing occasionally. My memory is maybe faulty, but I think we sang songs like "O Suzanna," "On Top of Old Smokey," "The Biscuits in the Army," "A Bicycle Built for Two," and a few Christian hymns mixed in like maybe "Amazing Grace" and "How Great Thou Art" if my memory is correct. I enjoyed the singing. It's perhaps the time in my life that I enjoyed singing most.

She had a copy of the Ten Commandments on the wall among several other things as I recall, though she seldom if ever referred to it. But I liked seeing it there.

Though I didn't attend church most of this time, I was blessed with wonderful friends who did. My best friend at Runyon (though I was blessed with several friends who could almost qualify as best friends) who seemed to be a fine Christian invited me to church multiple times. I asked him if it was within walking distance or if his mom would take me. He said his mom would take me once, and he said my mom would take me. I think I said I'd rather go with him, and asked if it was within walking distance. I think he went to the Church of Christ. It might have done me good if I'd gone with him.

I also remember sometimes reading literature left at our house by Jehovah's Witnesses. I enjoyed reading some of the articles in their publications and hoped they would bring them more regularly.

I also had friends who attended a Methodist Church, a Free Will Baptist Church, and a Mormon Church (Church of Jesus Christ of Latter-day Saints).

One of my many interests as a child was things about Kentucky. I enjoyed reading about Kentucky and liked Abraham Lincoln perhaps at least partially because he was the only President of the United States from Kentucky. I considered myself a Republican as a child perhaps at least partially for that reason. My dad being a Republican may have been a factor too. Mom seldom voted, but I think she was registered as a Democrat. In my fourth grade political discussions with classmates I supported Republican Richard Nixon vs. Democrat Robert Kennedy who then appeared to be the likely Democratic nominee for the 1968 Presidential election.

In the fifth grade, I continued to support Nixon. My friends and I got into several discussions about the election. Most of my classmates were Democrats. We had a mock vote in Ms. Williamson's fifth grade class. The Democratic candidate, Hubert H. Humphrey, got 16 votes [Kennedy had been assassinated], the independent candidate George Wallace got 9 votes, and Richard Nixon only got 3 votes, including mine. Nixon, of course, won the real election though.

One day when I was old enough to know better, I wrote on the dining room wall. When mom saw it, she was upset. She ordered me to sit at the dining room table till she got it off. She added that she would make me get it off myself, but she didn't think I could.

At first I was upset that she made me wait. As it took longer, and she seemed to be struggling with difficulty to remove the markings, I felt sorry for her. Then as it took even longer, I was afraid she wouldn't get it off before dad got home, or at least wouldn't get it off in time to cook supper before he got there.

I started praying. Then soon after I started praying, mom said something like, "There's one other thing I could try that I haven't tried." She went into the kitchen and got another cleaner, and quickly removed the stains from the wall. I considered it an answer to prayer.

I remember collecting baseball cards in the fifth grade and discussing Cincinnati Reds baseball with one of my friends who was a big fan. I remember having lots of fun, interesting discussions with classmates on various subjects during the fifth grade. I was blessed with several good friends, interested in a variety of things.

I remember one day Ms. Williamson asked for a volunteer to say the Pledge of Allegiance. I volunteered and said it. After I finished Ms. Williamson complimented me, then mentioned that I'd omitted two words and asked if anyone knew what they were.

Someone mentioned "under God" and she said that was right. I was surprised to learn I'd omitted them, since I knew they were in the pledge. I was slightly embarrassed, but neither my teacher nor any of the students made a big deal about it. We seemed to be blessed with an especially nice class. Miss Williamson and that fifth grade class are probably my favorite of all my classes in school.

In recent years there have been protests over the pledge. While I respect the pledge, including the two words "under God," I've written a revised pledge that I think may be more appropriate. It is included in a later chapter of this book along with some of my other writings. I've written on a very diverse group of topics.

On a related issue about the pledge, at a PTA meeting I attended with mom during my elementary school years at Runyon Elementary, someone (perhaps the PTA president?) asked me to lead in the pledge of allegiance, which I did. He then asked me to lead in something else, and I told him I didn't know the words to it. It was some patriotic song.

In case my pencil lead broke, I brought an extra

pencil to class. Sometimes someone who didn't have a pencil would ask to borrow one. I started bringing two extra ones, so I could give one away and still have an extra.

But, sometimes two people asked to borrow one, and I still didn't have an extra one after giving the two out. Eventually I started selling extra pencils, as well as other school supplies to classmates. But I still gave away some pencils to others who said they couldn't buy one because they didn't have any money. Sadly, there were apparently several poor students. Ms. Williamson may have given out pencils to some students too. And at least once classmate did besides me.

Ms. Williamson occasionally had parties for us, providing treats. One time when we were going to have a party, I remember a girl in my class saying to Ms. Williamson that Ms. Williamson always brought all the stuff for our parties and her mom had told her to ask if she could bring something to the party. Ms. Williamson said no, she would bring everything. The student asked why. Ms. Williamson hesitated, then she said she'd tell us the reason.

I'll paraphrase what my teacher said, as I remember it. Ms. Williamson told us that when she was a fairly new teacher, one time she was having a class party and told everyone to bring something, whatever they wanted for the party. One person didn't bring anything. When it was time for the party, that person just folded a sheet of paper into a cup and asked permission to go to the water fountain and get a cup of water. And that's all that person had. Other children poked fun at that person, laughed at them.

Ms. Williamson looked at my class and said, I don't think any of you would do that, but I will still bring everything to the party.

I was thinking I couldn't make a sheet of paper into a cup, and that the student who made that cup was gifted. One of the other students said that out loud.

I was also thinking that instead of having each student bring his or her own items, volunteers could have brought stuff for everyone. Although I didn't say it out loud, I felt that Ms. Williamson read my thoughts, and she suddenly realized that was something she could have done for that class years ago.

As Ms. Williamson told the story about that student who had been mocked in one of her previous classes, I had tears forming in my eyes. Embarrassed, I turned my head away to my left so my teacher couldn't see them.

After I did, I saw a girl in I think the first row on the left speak to another girl near her, saying something like, "Look at James. He's got tears in his eyes. That's what I like about him, not that he wins spelling bees or arithmetic matches or is a Republican or sells or gives away pencils to people that need them. Well, his giving away pencils to those who can't afford them is part of it. He cares about people. He's the man I'm going to marry. Well, probably not him, because he's interested in someone else and someone else is interested in him though she's not in our class this year, not the same person. But, he's not interested in me. But, I want to marry someone like him."

I had been embarrassed initially that the girl had noticed my tears, but then was flattered at her comments to the other girl. In the fifth grade I was indeed infatuated with one particular girl whom I spent much time staring at, as I was going through the early stages of puberty. She didn't seem interested in me though.

In the sixth grade I was still interested in that girl, as well as at least one other one. I didn't feel the initial one was interested in me, and didn't trust the other one's judgment based on what I knew of her. To make a long story short, it didn't work out with either of them. And I wasn't particularly interested in the girls that showed special interest in me. However, I considered everyone a friend.

By early 1971 when I was in the seventh grade at Runyon, I had decided that I wasn't going to get married until after I graduated college, and wasn't going to get engaged or serious with any girl at least until my first year of college, because I felt I might meet someone in high school or college that I felt more suitable as a spouse than anyone I knew at the time. I think I'd read in a Sunday newspaper article or in *Reader's Digest* that many/most persons who had girlfriends or boyfriends before college broke up with them after meeting someone new in college.

In the sixth grade on the standardized tests given to students I guess nationwide, my homeroom teacher Ms. Williamson said I made a perfect score on the spelling test, putting me at a high school senior level. My math teacher (Mr. Leland Cool) said my sixth grade score on the math standardized test was the best in my class, probably better than any of the seventh graders' scores, and comparable to the best eighth graders' scores at Runyon. I was pleasantly surprised. But I tried not to let it go to my head. I knew that we all have strengths and weaknesses. As mentioned earlier, I was terrible at art, and my handwriting was poor.

If I remember correctly, dad told me once that he'd talked to Mr. Williamson the principal about me skipping a grade and asked me if I'd be interested in that if it worked out. I told dad I wasn't interested in it. I had many friends among my classmates and felt I'd be in over my head socially among those a grade higher.

However, during the seventh grade, we had what was called grade-level classes for some subjects. I was with primarily eighth graders in math class and science class. I did well in Mr. Leland Cool's top level math class, possibly still being the best student.

Science was another story. In the sixth and seventh grades with Mr. Buford Cool (I think my math teacher Leland Cool and my science teacher Buford Cool were brothers.) as my science teacher, I found he got into much more depth than my earlier teachers in science. Furthermore, he didn't use a textbook or handouts. That made things more difficult for me. I often learned better from reading than verbal instructions. I can reread difficult passages while skimming those I know or consider unimportant.

My note taking wasn't very good. In my seventh grade advanced science class primarily with eighth graders, when he devoted what seemed like several days to discussing pulley systems, either drawing them on the blackboard or often just making a display on his desk, I couldn't draw them accurately in my notes or memorize them. And I felt they weren't that important. He had a book on his desk that he looked at before drawing or modeling them. I felt like saying to him "I may never need to make a pulley system. But if you'd just give us printed copies of them all, I'd file them on a bookshelf to refer to if necessary." But I never said it.

I struggled much in science in that seventh grade class. Mr. Buford Cool's approach of not using a textbook, not giving handouts, and often focusing on subjects that interested me little made it tough. Being with primarily eighth graders made it tougher.

There was also a rumor of alleged cheating by other students, and I was told they were doing an undercover investigation to try to catch the culprits in the act. We moved away while I was still in the seventh grade. I don't know if cheating was found and proven in the investigation or not. At any rate, I earned my grade honestly. And for various reasons, my science grades were not good overall in that class.

I did learn much in his class though, especially when he focused on subjects that interested me, even though I fell short of my potential. My favorite times in his class though were when he digressed a bit into intelligent comments on issues.

I remember one day in particular when he stated something like that he believed virtually all things went in cycles. He said he thought that applied to intelligence too. He stated that though we had major scientific advancements in recent years only a few people understood them and he felt the majority of persons were becoming less intelligent. Either he said or I got the impression that someday the electric grid including the electric lighting systems would be so perfect that one person could operate it, then that one person would pass on to heaven, and the world would be in the dark again. I found that thought-provoking.

In hindsight, I would like to have worked on the school newspaper under his leadership. He was the faculty member who oversaw the school newspaper. I considered applying to join the newspaper in the 7th grade, but only saw solicitations for sports reporter and gossip columnist on a paper given out to our class about various extracurricular activities, including working on the school newspaper. I was interested in news.

However, an incident later in the 7th grade led me to believe he desired to change the newspaper to focus more on investigative reporting and news reporting. Furthermore, the 8th grade student who served as the newspaper editor told me specifically that Mr. Cool would be talking with me soon about working for the school newspaper, possibly even being the editor for the following year, when I would be in the 8th grade. However, we moved away soon after that, so who knows what would have happened?

One of the things I enjoyed doing at Stone was shooting my BB gun. Bobby, a young neighbor, perhaps five years old, begged me to let him shoot it. I told him about gun safety, never to point it at someone, including himself, and that even if it appeared to be empty a BB might be caught in the chamber. Then I let him shoot it, with me partially holding the gun.

Some time later, mom told me that the boy's grandmother had told her that one day her husband, the boy's grandfather, was cleaning his gun, either a rifle or a shotgun, I'm not sure which. The grandfather looked down the barrel of the gun to see how it looked.

The boy told him not to do that; he might shoot himself. The grandfather told him the gun was empty. The boy said a bullet might be caught in the chamber even though it seemed empty. When the grandfather asked how he knew about guns, the boy mentioned me teaching him. The grandmother told mom the boy might have saved his grandfather's life.

I was late developing in certain ways. For example, I was older than my friends in learning to ride a bicycle without training wheels. I was reluctant to try it.

But one day dad went out onto the clubhouse lawn with me and held my bicycle up while I started riding it without training wheels, and he let go. I was riding it. I was surprised at how easy it was.

I try to always be truthful, but sometimes I fall short. And while dad was teaching me how to ride without training wheels, one or some of my friends came up. One asked if dad was teaching me how to ride without training wheels. I lied and said no, I guess due to embarrassment.

I was also older than my playmates when I stopped believing in Santa Claus, though I had doubts and some disbelief at a young age. I remember discussing Santa Claus with mom in the kitchen one day while one of my friends was there. He told mom if she didn't tell me the truth, one of my friends would soon, adding I think that it wouldn't be him. Mom then told me the truth.

I began reading newspapers at an early age and clipping clippings from them too. I still have clippings dating back to December 1968 when I was 10 years old. Two of the early ones dealt with the newly elected President Nixon who was soon to take office. I saved numerous clippings related to the passing on of former President Dwight David Eisenhower on Friday, March 28th, 1969. Based on the clippings, I was impressed with Eisenhower.

I also saved lots of clippings about the Apollo space program, including Apollo 11 which included the first landing of human beings on the moon. I remember enjoying watching on television the first landing on the moon, which took place during the summer of 1969, after I had completed the fifth grade.

I also saved several clippings about odd or unusual events/stories. I've been fascinated by such stories since childhood. I remain so.

The newspapers dad subscribed to during part or all of my childhood included at least one or two weeklies and at least three daily newspapers. The dailies were The Louisville *Courier-Journal*, the Huntington, West Virginia *Herald-Dispatch*, and the Williamson, West Virginia *Williamson Daily News*. The Williamson paper did not publish on Sundays.

I also read magazines and books. Dad subscribed to at least a few magazines.

I loved to read. As mentioned earlier, I especially enjoyed mystery novels. I read books like the Hardy

Boys books, Nancy Drew, Brains Benton, Trixie Belden, The Power Boys, etc. I enjoyed reading Civil War history too. And I read/skimmed several of the small orange-covered biographies in the Runyon Elementary School library. And I ordered a lot of books through book clubs at school.

One day when one of my friends at Stone and I were in my bedroom, he suggested I read other books than mysteries, since I primarily read mystery books. He stated that though I'd read a lot of books, he had perhaps read a wider variety.

Among the ones he mentioned that could be beneficial to read was Benjamin Franklin's autobiography. He said the autobiography was written in simple language and included a section with a list of areas of one's life to improve on. He said he'd tried applying the principles, but not doing each for a week as the book indicated Franklin did. He said having an accountability partner seeking to do the same thing might help him and me both.

He also mentioned a science fiction book series that was expected to have the third book of in a sense a trilogy finished soon, which I think was the *Dune* series. He said reading the first book in the series really made him feel like he was in that place due to the descriptions, and though he hadn't liked the second book as well, he thought the third was to be more like the first.

I regret not taking his advice to read more diversely. But I have been seeking to correct that in recent years. I did read Benjamin Franklin's autobiography and now seek to follow Franklin's guidelines, modified for myself. And, I have read a much wider variety of things, including the Dune series. Even at Stone though, I read some astronomy, history, biography, newspapers, magazines, etc.

Sometimes my friends would come up to visit, and sometimes they'd phone before coming up. But mom told me to never go in my friends' houses without her permission. And once when I was going to phone a friend, she said not to, if he wanted to come up he'd phone me.

I remember playing with my friend Brian Egan at his house not long after the Martin Luther King, Jr. assassination. The television was on in the living room where we were playing, and it showed a replay of the assassination and discussed it. I had seen it several times before. I told Brian that I didn't remember hearing of King before the assassination, but he must have been a very important person from the way the media was focusing on it.

Brian stated that he'd heard of him because Thelma (their maid) talked about him, but he'd heard a lot more about him recently since the assassination. He added that Thelma was off work on this particular day, and if she had been there working that day he'd have had to turn the television off or switch the channel, because every time it came on, she started crying. I asked him why. Brian said he wasn't sure, he didn't know. He said he'd asked his dad, and his dad told him it was because Thelma thought all her dreams were ending; she didn't know they were just beginning.

Runyon Elementary School was basically

segregated, as was Stone Camp. I only remember seeing three African-Americans close up on a regular basis in Stone Camp or in my classes at Runyon Elementary School. One was Thelma, the maid for the Egan family, whom I mentioned earlier, and who seemed to be a wonderful person. Another was the ice cream man who came around regularly in the summer. He also seemed friendly and a wonderful person. The third was an African-American who enrolled in the school, who seemed to be a nice person too. All three were positive role models.

Occasionally I would stay overnight with friends at Stone or they would stay overnight with me. On one of these occasions, I was staying with my friend Brian Egan. After Brian and I were in bed, his dad came in to hear his prayers. Brian, apparently embarrassed, asked if his dad could skip them this night since I was there. His dad replied no, and I might even want to say mine too. I enjoyed hearing Brian say his prayers aloud in the presence of his dad.

I didn't say any prayers that night and was too embarrassed to tell Brian's dad that I never said evening prayers. However, sometime afterward, as a result of that, I began saying an evening prayer. I've continued the practice almost every night since. For some years, I've also sought to regularly enjoy a morning prayer and to try to remain in a prayerful spirit throughout the day.

Brian's family attended the Church of Jesus Christ of Latter-day Saints. After his retirement as a mining engineer, Brian's dad, Howard Egan became even more active in the church, and one of the relatively high level officials in the denomination. Mr. Egan impressed me as a compassionate, intelligent person. He was the chief engineer, my dad's supervisor, too.

I remember one day some of my friends talking about the movie *2001: A Space Odyssey* which Brian's dad had taken them to see. I wasn't asked, unless they asked my mom and/or dad and they said no. Based on my limited memory of what one of my playmates said afterward, Brian's dad had apparently indicated the movie symbolized what life was all about, perhaps a progression toward perfection, or something like that.

I had other playmates that went to a Methodist Church and a Free Will Baptist Church. Though I didn't attend church at the time, as I remember it I basically tried to be a "good" person, truthful, honest, etc. But I know I fell short. We all do.

I remember hiking in the Red River Gorge area with dad, including the Rock Bridge trail, which had small plaques near some of the trees identifying them. We also hiked to Sky Bridge and Natural Bridge, as well as Chimney Top Rock, and other areas. I remember us driving through the Nada tunnel. I enjoyed the hiking and talking with dad about various things.

One of the purposes of dad's trips was his search for John Swift's silver mines and/or silver. But I enjoyed the hiking and fellowship. We never found any silver or a silver mine on any of the trips I took with dad. But I enjoyed the fellowship much. As I got older and dad's trips included what I considered dangerous cave explorations, I seldom went with him.

My paternal grandfather, Edwin Joseph Gibson,

whom I called Grondy, passed on while we lived at Stone. After he passed on, I remember when mom and I were going through some letters and papers in the house he had rented, I found some envelopes addressed to him in Jenkins from decades earlier. Mom said not to tell dad, because it might alter him. She said he might move to Jenkins although he's not supposed to or he might not move there though he's supposed to. My mom said that Mrs. Gibson (dad's mom, Edwin Joseph Gibson's wife) who had passed on in 1963 had told my mom that she wasn't sure if dad was supposed to move to Jenkins or not. We did move to Jenkins some years later when I was a junior in high school.

During the time we lived in Stone, we did most of our shopping in nearby Williamson, West Virginia as I mentioned earlier. Williamson seemed like a city to me. It had two 5 & 10 cent stores, R.H. Hobbs and G.C. Murphy. I didn't know of another town with two of them. It had a bookstore, The Book Nook, that I enjoyed visiting. It had Michael's which sold comic books and paperback books, among other things. There was the Cinderella movie theatre. A large Sears department store was there. And there was at least one shoe store where mom bought me shoes. There were clothing stores, too. Mom bought a lot of stuff at the Sundry Store though I typically didn't.

Mom and I both checked books out of the Williamson Public Library. There was an A & P supermarket. Across the river from Williamson in South Williamson, Kentucky there was a Kroger supermarket.

Williamson had a huge number of railroad tracks,

perhaps 15 or 20, used for coal haulage/storage. There was even a building made out of coal in Williamson, referred to as the Coal House. Williamson held a Christmas parade each year, which was in the evening. And I remember going to it at least once.

Mom was reluctant for us to go to an indoor theatre during mine and my sister's early childhood, feeling we'd misbehave I guess. I think the first movie we saw at an indoor theater was *Gone With the Wind* at the Cinderella Theatre in Williamson, West Virginia. It had a four-letter word at the end, but mom said a neighbor recommended it highly despite that. I found the movie entertaining.

After *Gone With the Wind*, our family saw several other movies at theatres during my elementary and high school years, mainly Disney comedy movies. I especially enjoyed *The Love Bug* and *Blackbeard's Ghost*.

As I got into my latter years of elementary school I watched television less. We typically got three different programs, one on each of the three major television networks at the time: ABC, CBS, and NBC.

In addition to reading, I often listened to the radio on a clock radio that I received from dad and mom as a present. I remember seeking to find out how many different radio stations I could pick up. I wanted to make a complete list. And I did. At night after the local stations signed off, I could pick up stations from much of the eastern United States. I discuss my radio listening more later in this book.

The Vietnam War was going on while we lived at Stone. I remember worrying about whether I would be drafted and if I'd be too scared to go if I was. At the time, I didn't think of the ethics of the war. I just assumed that the United States was correct.

Mom told me not to worry, that the war might be over before I became old enough to be drafted. It was.

I remember especially two scenes from the evening television network news Vietnam War coverage. One was a case where before showing the video, we viewers were repeatedly warned that it was not a simulation and was graphic. The video that followed on the newscast showed the execution of one of the enemy via someone holding a pistol near his head and firing.

I disliked the scene, and said to my dad who was also watching, something like "I thought those were the good guys." He replied something like, "They are, that was a quick and painless death without torture." After a short pause, I think dad added something like "they may have tortured him before, but there's no indication of it. He seemed in nice shape."

The other scene I remember from Vietnam War network news coverage took place when video coverage from the front became color. Many programs including the news were in color before the video footage from the war zone became color instead of black and white.

The first time they showed color footage from the Vietnam War zone, I was astounded at the beautiful bright green forests. I said to mom and dad something like "those forests look as good as the ones here in southeastern Kentucky," and I was wondering if since the forests were the same, the people might be. Dad seemed to be reading my thoughts and stated something like

"And the people there are just like the people here too."

I began to rethink the ethics of the war.

While I was in elementary school I became a fan of University of Kentucky basketball and football. The first game I remember watching was the 1970 NCAA basketball tournament game between Kentucky with its star player, All-American Dan Issel, and Jacksonville with its star, Artis Gilmore. I cried after Kentucky lost.

I remain a UK fan, as do many others here in Kentucky. In the early 1970s few games were on television, so listening to Cawood Ledford call the games on the radio was my main way of following them, in addition to reading newspaper articles.

As I mentioned earlier, I loved the 1960s Batman television show. I remember watching an episode where a villain turned Batman's cape pink. I told dad and mom that Batman's cape doesn't look pink on our television screen. Mom or dad stated that's because we have a black and white television. For some reason, I hadn't thought about that. Dad said it might be time for us to get a color television, so we could see scenes like that in color. I think it was soon after that when our family got its first color television.

I remember watching the "Hissoner the Penguin" episode of Batman with dad, liking Batman's campaign style, feeling he was doing it the right way and that dad would agree.

Dad who was watching with me, then stated something like "Batman is doing it the right way, but I don't know if that would work in real life." Then, when a scene of a nearly empty Batman campaign headquarters was shown, dad said something like "See how few people that are there at Batman headquarters compared to the Penguin's."

By February 1971, I was feeling a bit isolated from some of my friends, partially due to the amount of time I devoted to studying for the spelling team probably. It was also possibly due to mom apparently being stricter than any of the other moms in the camp were. I wasn't allowed to go some of the places they went.

In hindsight this may have been a blessing. Already being away from my friends much of the time made it easier to move away from them. It kept me out of trouble too. At any rate, I had mixed emotions, but I wasn't too upset when dad and mom decided to move from Stone to Phelps due to dad accepting a new job.

Chapter 4: Finishing Grade School and High School

Living at Phelps (Middle of Seventh Grade to Middle of High School Junior Year)

In February 1971 when I was in the seventh grade we moved from Stone to Phelps.

Even before we moved to Phelps, I was becoming I think more introverted and shy. That continued at Phelps. I read a lot, watched a TV in my bedroom that I received as a gift, listened to the radio, hiked the area near our house some, and shot my bb gun.

Folks at Phelps school welcomed me as a newcomer, as I was welcomed in other towns we moved to. I won in my class in checkers games, was the key to the boys winning an arithmetic match, and won at paper football against everyone I played except for one girl. I think some people deliberately lost to me to make me feel good and welcome me to the school. But I did do well. And I enjoyed some nice friendships.

At the time we moved to Phelps when I was in the seventh grade, the English class at Phelps had already started on a term paper. The teacher, Mrs. Compton, showed me a list of possible topics to choose from. I chose one that interested me, "Campus Violence."

They'd already done much preparatory work like using the library for research in the *Readers' Guide to Periodical Literature*, etc. At the time I knew little about library research and hadn't even heard of the *Readers' Guide to Periodical Literature*. I researched back issues of *Look* and *Readers Digest* magazines that dad and mom subscribed to. My teacher wrote "Good paper A" on my term paper which was 16 pages (including the bibliography page, but excluding the table of contents page). I still have it. The date on it indicates I turned it in on April 23, 1971. I was pleased with the grade, her comment, and as I recall enjoyed the writing of the paper.

I liked doing the term paper at Phelps much better than much of the stuff we'd been doing in my 7th grade English class at Runyon, such as diagramming sentences. I felt diagramming sentences was a waste of time. Even if learning the parts of speech is important (and I realize its importance now), I thought and still think there are better ways to learn them than by diagramming sentences.

I haven't diagrammed a sentence since my seventh grade days at Runyon. However, diagramming was one approach toward better learning the parts of speech. Maybe some others benefited more from it than I did. With more dedication, I could likely have learned more from it.

In the eighth grade, my English teacher, Mr. Daugherty, showed us a huge list of possible careers, allowing us to pick five to learn more about. My first choice was freelance writer. Even as I selected it #1, I knew that its job opportunities were limited, pay was low, and competition was tough. My other four selections were more "practical."

My freshman class at Phelps High School included students from three grade schools: Phelps, Freeburn, and Majestic. I was voted President of my high school freshman class. I considered it quite an honor.

I tried to be friendly and fair to everyone and considered everyone a friend. My understanding is that I got votes in the election from all three schools. I confess that I did little as class president though. I knew little about the job responsibilities and took little initiative.

My freshman English class was taught by Mrs. Compton who was now a high school teacher after being my seventh grade English teacher earlier. In my freshman English class, we had a debate on capital punishment. I was not willing to debate on the side I disagreed with, so I would not have been a good candidate for the high school debate team. For the same reason I doubt I'd have been a good law school student. Perhaps ironically, I was initially opposed to capital punishment, then moments later decided I was definitely for it, and chose that side. My best friend in the class argued the other side. We had a few others in our group in addition to the two of us. But he and I did most of the talking. He argued against capital punishment and I argued in favor of it. Now, I am opposed to capital punishment as a general rule. I loved the debating.

In that freshman English class, we also subdivided into groups for a writing project. Each group was responsible for writing an English grammar book. Our group's 93 page book was titled *An Easy Way to Make an A in English*. We received an A- on it. I got permission to keep my group's "book" and still have it.

In my sophomore English class we had some enjoyable literature readings and discussions. In terms of overall enjoyment, that was probably my favorite high school class. Mr. Jack Cunningham led us in nice discussions and taught us about literature in a way other English teachers hadn't.

In a blog entry I posted on Google Blogger on March 4, 2018, I wrote about an incident that occurred during my junior year at Phelps High School in 1974. One day my American history teacher, J.C. Young, stated something like "Multiple nations possess atomic weapons. But only one nation has ever used them in war against another nation. Do you know which country it was?"

Several persons shook their heads that they didn't know or remained silent. But at least a few said it was Russia (the Soviet Union). Though I am ignorant about many things, I had begun reading newspapers, magazines, and books regularly at an early age. I knew it was the United States and spoke up saying so. I think a few persons nodded or spoke quietly that I was right. Perhaps they already knew but had kept quiet.

But, a person on the other side of the room spoke up loudly that it wasn't the United States or Russia, but was Japan, adding that we all ought to always remember the day the Japanese dropped the atomic bomb on Pearl Harbor. I think a few of her friends seated near her quietly corrected her, and I think she was embarrassed and recognized her mistake.

Deep inside, I think most of us probably knew that the United States is the only country to use such weapons, dropping them on Hiroshima and Nagasaki, Japan in August 1945 to end WWII. However, it shocked me that so many others provided incorrect information initially.

Often we speak (or write) without thinking clearly. Also, our views can be distorted by misleading information or "fake news." Though it wasn't me that day, several other times I've misspoken myself. Indeed, you'll probably find lots of typos in this book—maybe some egregious errors too, though I hope not.

In fairness to my fellow students, the Cold War between the Soviet Union/Russia and the United States was going on during our childhood. That was probably a factor in many fellow students' views that Russia was responsible for using atomic weapons.

The Vietnam War was also going on during my early childhood as I mentioned earlier. I was fearful during elementary school of being drafted and of being afraid to serve if I was drafted. At the time, I didn't think about the morals of the war or the possibility of the U.S. being wrong. I just assumed we were right.

Patriotism seems especially common among hillbillies (I like either the term Appalachian-Americans or hillbillies.). My view of the Vietnam War changed later, possibly even before I finished elementary school. I'm basically a pacifist now. Somehow, I feel we need to find ways to resolve all conflicts fairly and peacefully.

In addition to reading and writing, conflict resolution is a subject that has interested me since childhood. Seeking to learn about conflict resolution is perhaps one reason I enjoyed attending seminars and lectures after I enrolled in college at the University of Kentucky. Often the topics were controversial subjects in the news.

Due to the Appalachian mountains limiting

television reception, the coal mining towns in southeastern Kentucky may have been among the first places in the country to get cable television. However, the cable television systems in southeastern Kentucky in the 1950s, 1960s, and 1970s when I was growing up only offered 3-5 channels. As I mentioned earlier, often we only had three programs to choose from, one on ABC, one on CBS, and one on NBC. For things like Presidential addresses, all channels provided the same live broadcast.

Though I watched television some, often I read or listened to the radio instead both in elementary school and high school. As I noted earlier, after mom and dad gave me a clock radio as a gift for either my birthday or Christmas while I was in elementary school, I devoted some time to seeing how many different radio stations I could pick up. I found that in the evening I could pick up stations from much of the eastern United States. I listed all of them. A wide variety of radio programming was available.

I enjoyed the diversity of the programming and learning little tidbits of information.

One station I listened to a lot was WHAS in Louisville. In addition to broadcasting University of Kentucky basketball and football games, as well as Kentucky Colonels American Basketball Association professional basketball games which I sometimes listened to, it featured a radio call-in show hosted by Milton Metz.

Metz hosted a wide variety of guests on his program. He encouraged listeners to phone in with comments and questions. Milton Metz impressed me with his even temperament and his willingness to allow views on either side of issues to be expressed. He rarely if ever injected his personal view. It rarely was even clear which side he was on; he seemed neutral.

At night WHAS's signal could apparently be picked up in much of the eastern United States. Milton Metz's audience reflected that. Calls sometimes came from areas far from Kentucky.

Current national radio and television talk show hosts would benefit if they tried to behave more like him on the air. I still think he's the best radio talk show host I've ever heard. Of course I've only heard a relatively few.

I also enjoyed listening sometimes to the CBS Radio Mystery Theatre. It began in 1974 and was also broadcast on WHAS, which was then a CBS affiliate. The show gave me an idea of what it was like during my parents' childhoods before television when they probably listened to radio programs similar to our watching television programs now. I actually enjoyed listening to a radio program and visualizing the scenes in my mind rather than just seeing them on a television screen.

While we lived at Phelps, mom became pregnant with my sister Deborah (Deb). Deb was born in 1974, completing our family of five.

Due to dad changing jobs, we moved from Phelps during my junior year of high school. This was perhaps the toughest of my childhood moves.

I didn't want to leave my friends, especially my best friend with whom I enjoyed a lot of what I considered thought-provoking, intelligent conversations about various issues, including politics, the environment, education, and morals.

He and I also studied together some. I helped him in algebra. He was my lab partner in biology and chemistry and helped me in those areas. I did well in the textbook part of biology and chemistry, but I wasn't that good at lab, especially biology lab.

Living at Jenkins the First Time (Middle of High School Junior Year Until Leaving for College)

My family moved from Phelps to Jenkins during my junior year of high school in November 1974. Before the move I inventoried my stuff and numbered the cardboard boxes most of it was packed in. Looking at the list in the inventory notebook for each box, I could see what was in most of them.

Though I felt bad about moving away from my friends at Phelps, and it was probably my hardest move of those we made during my childhood, I adapted. One key is that I was welcomed into Jenkins as at other places. Students and teachers welcomed me.

I especially remember the friendliness of my geometry teacher, Mr. Bentley. Math had been my best subject in school. As I mentioned earlier, in second grade a teacher picked me to show some students in a class a few years older how to do a problem. In sixth grade, I performed the best in my class on standardized tests, and the teacher said I outperformed the seventh graders too, and was comparable to the best eighth graders at Runyon Elementary School. Also, as a high school algebra student at Phelps I showed a substitute teacher how to do a problem that she requested help on.

But at Jenkins, they were studying different things in geometry than my class at Phelps had been, using a different textbook. I had some catching up to do.

Mr. Bentley offered me guidance. Indeed, the way he seemed to show individual interest in each student in the class impressed me. God blessed me with many wonderful teachers. But, to the best of my memory, none of my other high school teachers at either Phelps or Jenkins demonstrated that personal touch to the same degree to their students that he did.

Though my passion lay in reading and writing, math was my best subject. Mr. Bentley helped me further develop my math skills during my junior geometry class, as well as my senior class in solid geometry and trigonometry which he also taught.

When mom and I were checking in at Jenkins High School, the guidance counselor (Mr. Belcher) said I was probably going to be the valedictorian. I was surprised and told him that I thought someone had to go to a school all four years to be eligible for that award. He said no, there was no regulation. It, of course, would depend on how the rest of my junior year and my senior year went.

The guidance counselor also asked about my college plans. I had never told anyone before what I planned to major in. But I had been leaning toward an engineering undergraduate degree, followed by an MBA, with electives in other areas.

I told Mr. Belcher that I planned to major in mining engineering and get an MBA. I'd initially decided as a freshman in high school to major in engineering and then get an MBA since a book in the Phelps library indicated that this combination offered quality job prospects in various areas.

However, my talking to Mr. Belcher that day was the first time I'd mentioned mining engineering or even engineering and an MBA to anyone if I remember correctly. He stated that mining engineering scholarships were available if I chose that path, and we could talk about that later. We did, and I received one.

As I had earlier at Phelps and Runyon, I sought to be friendly to everyone at Jenkins. I considered everyone a friend or potential friend.

I tried to talk to persons in various groups, rather than be part of a particular clique. And there were certain cliques or groups of students that related more closely with one another than with others at Jenkins, Phelps, Runyon, and I guess all schools.

At lunch, after eating I sometimes went to Mr. Cook's room where a few friends gathered during lunch. Vernard Whitaker and others welcomed me into their group. We sometimes played chess. To make it a fast-paced game for the limited time available, time per move was supposed to be short. I often took too long due to my desire to make the right move. I was probably a negative influence on the short lunch chess matches.

During my early childhood, years before we moved to Jenkins, I had visited Jenkins with dad multiple times. As I mentioned elsewhere, dad had devoted much of his spare time to searching for John Swift's silver mines. I sometimes accompanied him on his trips. And one place we visited multiple times was Jenkins.

I enjoyed seeing the Pine Mountain fault on the mountain beside the road leading from Jenkins to Virginia, and the unusual angle at which the rock formations lay. I enjoyed hiking to Raven Rock and looking at the view. I enjoyed seeing the blow hole where objects instead of dropping down into the hole, were held up due to out coming air (The hole did not blow any longer the last time I saw it, which was perhaps about ten years ago.). And I enjoyed going partway through a former railroad tunnel from Virginia to Kentucky near Jenkins. I entered on the Virginia side.

Furthermore, dad sometimes stopped at a mom and pop drive-in restaurant in Jenkins to eat. The restaurant is now closed. It was located near where Paul Baker's barbershop is now. I was usually hungry and enjoyed eating. Dad loved to eat tasty food. If near a place he liked to eat, such as that fast food restaurant in Jenkins, dad would stop.

If we weren't near a place dad liked to eat, he would often wait a long time until he got to one before stopping to eat. Many of the places we traveled to were in rural areas, apparently far from any type of restaurant. I learned to pack myself a snack. Sometimes both dad and I packed food.

Dad preferred restaurants that offered reasonably priced home cooked meals to fast food burger places when he could find them. One of those homestyle cooking restaurants he liked was in Stanton, Kentucky. Another was Opal and Joe's in Ivel. Both are now closed.

An additional thing I liked about Jenkins during our visits there was a large sign in the eastern part of

Jenkins on the roadside that stated something like "Jenkins, Kentucky, We're Proud to Be Kentuckians," which I think included an ad for RC Cola. I was proud to be a Kentuckian too.

Jenkins was probably my favorite place to visit among those dad and I traveled to as a child. I even suggested to dad one day after looking at the RC Cola "We're Proud to Be Kentuckians" sign that it would be nice to move to Jenkins.

I figured he'd say no, or laugh, but he seemed to respond seriously, "maybe someday" or something similar. I was surprised. I think I'd have been happier if we'd moved at that time, when I think I was still in elementary school, rather than years later during my junior year of high school.

I felt as a young child, and still feel, that Jenkins is a special place. In some ways it seems like a microcosm of the world. Once on a visit there after I'd moved to central Kentucky, as I approached Jenkins, I actually felt as if I were seeing a smaller version of the world. Then as I entered into Jenkins, the vision changed to a vision of being part of a small town.

Once a bustling relatively self-sufficient coal mining town of several thousand people, the town now (2020) probably has fewer than 2,000 people. But due to its geology, lake, a museum, a library, etc., it is nicer than typical coal mining towns. There's even a marvelous Civil War monument on top of Pound Mountain above Jenkins that pays tribute to both sides of the war. But every place I've visited or lived is nice and unique in its own way.

During my high school years at Phelps and Jenkins, I often stayed up late and I slept late. I didn't seem to get sleepy until late.

Often I got up just in time to dress and go to school. Mom would wake me up, then later holler up the stairs to ask if I was ready. I would reply, "I'm working on it." Sometimes I was still in bed, just barely starting to work on getting ready, if that, though. Mom typically drove me, Barb, and often another person or persons to school.

Sometimes they were already in the car when I was still in bed. But, as far as I remember, we were never late getting there. I typically skipped breakfast, and could dress, get my stuff, and get out to the car in only a few minutes. Fortunately, in college without mom there, I set alarm clocks and got myself up and to class.

During the latter part of my high school years, I also did a little babysitting of my sister Deb. It was the first time I'd spent much time around a baby that small that I remember. I was only three years old when my other sister Barbara was born, and didn't remember when she was a baby. I enjoyed babysitting Deb. I never changed a diaper, but I did do some other babysitting. She was still only two when I left for college. But on trips home from college, we played games, walked to the Post Office together, etc. It was fun for me, and she seemed to enjoy it much too.

My senior year at Jenkins High School was an unusual year in some respects. Bomb threats led to us being sent home early several times. Fortunately no bombs were found.

My physics teacher, Mr. Cook, was also a school bus driver and often left physics class to drive a school bus for the grades that dismissed before high school students. We covered little physics. And we seniors had a substitute teacher for English class much of the year as I recall.

Most of our class probably got most of our school education in our first 11 years of schooling. But we had a nice senior class in 1975-76. I think 52 persons were in our class, and eight of us went to the University of Kentucky. Several others went to other schools. Many of us earned scholarships.

Of course college is only one avenue to success. I loved the diversity of courses offered in college and the various extracurricular activities. But for persons seeking a career, a trade school, apprenticeship, on-the-job training, etc, offer alternatives. College is not for everyone. And persons who become carpenters, electricians, plumbers, etc., often make more per hour worked than many college-educated persons who devote themselves to careers as social workers, librarians, journalists, freelance writers, etc.

But the fulfillment that comes from enjoying one's work, finding it beneficial for oneself and others, and matching one's passions, interests, and aptitudes is key. I felt and still feel that my love for reading and writing made a university education an excellent fit for me. However, alternatives may be better for a lot of people.

As it turned out, I was selected as the valedictorian of Jenkins High School's class of 1976. I was also voted male "most likely to succeed" by my classmates, and I was awarded the mathematics award and the Kiwanis award. I was also awarded a mining engineering scholarship. And I was runner up for the American Legion Award, which I think Mike Vanover won. Mike was a wonderful person and very deserving of the award as I see it.

When I wrote my valedictory speech, I initially included a phrase offering thanks to "most of all God." But, even though I said a prayer each night, I did not go to church and was in a sense perhaps an agnostic. I felt it would be thought wrong if I said "most of all God" since I didn't go to church, though I did have a sort of belief in God and enjoyed my evening prayers, getting an answer at times from God, my own inner thoughts, ESP from another person, or some other source.

I guess you could say I was an agnostic who thought God might exist and it was best to behave as if God did. I strongly supported righteous moral living, and in a sense probably had a form of faith in God as an agnostic, if that makes sense.

I prayed about it, and I felt the Holy Spirit saying through an inner voice to omit the phrase "most of all God," from my valedictory speech, which I did. Instead, I wrote and then later said at the graduation ceremony "most of all our parents" as part of my speech.

One day during my senior year, some of the top academic students in the high school were selected to spend some time one day in the gym free from classes. I was never really an athlete. I took some books to read during this time. I took several so I could pick whichever

I was in the mood to read on at a particular time.

I remember the guidance counselor, Mr. Belcher, coming up to me and talking about my books. He specifically mentioned one called *Strictly Speaking: Will American Be the Death of English?* by Edwin Newman and read briefly from it, citing my deep reading. I told him some of my other books were lighter reading, which they were.

The guidance counselor may have been inferring that I might be more interested in a career related to writing or law or something other than mining engineering. But if so, I didn't pick up on it.

Shortly after the guidance counselor spoke, one of the other high school students who was in the gym and sitting near me complimented me on the variety of books I had. Then that student noted that none of them dealt with mining engineering.

I said something like, "I'll read about that in college." The other student said something like "I know that, but I thought you might want to read about that now to prepare for college, that is if mining engineering is really what you want to do." The student's comment was thought-provoking. That student seemed to have an insight I lacked. As I thought about it, I felt I didn't feel that passionate about mining engineering. But I had a mining engineering scholarship, and decided to stick with my plans.

Attending high school football and basketball sporting events was a major leisure time activity in Jenkins for students, as it was at Phelps and probably is in most areas. However, I was not that interested in them.

Though I didn't follow high school sports, I was an avid University of Kentucky basketball and football fan, a weakness I still have to a lesser extent. Reading was probably my top leisure activity.

During my high school years, I had a few chores to do around the house. While at Jenkins, I carried in coal for the stoker for our coal furnace in cold weather. In warmer weather I mowed the grass and trimmed the hedges using a manual hedge trimmer.

Dad bought an electric hedge trimmer. But I preferred trimming the hedges with the manual one. It was lighter to hold. I didn't have to worry about the electrical cord getting in the way. And it was quieter. Due to its quietness, I could exchange greetings with neighbors as they walked by or drove by with their car windows down. I could also meditate and daydream.

One of the things I thought about was college. I looked forward to attending college. I was excited about the new opportunities that awaited there.

Chapter 5: My College Years and Early "Career" Years

Going to the University of Kentucky

During the seventh grade at Runyon Elementary School, I'd told a friend that I planned to attend the University of Kentucky. My plans did not change.

Dad and mom tried to convince me to attend a nearby community college for two years and drive back and forth to college instead of going to the University of Kentucky (UK) and staying in a dormitory. But I was determined to go to UK, and I had a scholarship that could pay much of the cost. I felt that UK was a larger school, had a nicer library, offered a wider variety of classes, and was better overall. I think I also wanted to be on my own away from dad and mom.

As a high school freshman at Phelps I think I'd read in school library book that UK had the best research library in the state of Kentucky, so I felt I could learn about a variety of things. I was also a UK basketball and football fan and looked forward to possibly attending their home games, but (I hope?) that was a secondary factor.

I heard dad tell mom on one occasion something like since I had that scholarship, it would be hard to stop me from going to UK.

The University of Kentucky mailed much information in advance about what to expect and how to prepare. I also had read articles in newspapers about beginning college. Dad also relayed some information from his experience.

In advance, I made out a lengthy packing list of items to take. I didn't want to forget anything. Dad and mom probably added some items to the list. We loaded up the station wagon with stuff. It was loaded.

I enjoyed being on my own in a sense. Some persons get homesick at college. Personally, I felt at home from my first day, as I remember. The summer preparations helped. I'm grateful to God, UK, dad, and mom for their roles in preparing me for the move. I enjoyed the privilege of having own mail box, a telephone shared only with my roommate, etc., though I didn't get that much mail or make or receive many calls.

My dorm was conveniently located near my classes, the UK student center, the campus book stores, and downtown Lexington. It was also near several Lexington city bus routes, so I could travel around much of the city relatively easily even though I didn't have a car.

Excited about starting college, in fall 1976 I began my studies at the University of Kentucky. During the summer of 1976 mom, dad, and I attended a summer advising conference that offered lots of information about what to expect on campus and a chance to see part of the campus. Also, I received lots of informative information via mail during the time between when I was accepted and when I enrolled, as I mentioned earlier.

As part of the summer advising conference, I think incoming students were requested to fill out an optional survey questionnaire for some organization about various things. One of the questions was about religion, and I listed myself as an agnostic. Though I said a prayer each evening, and tried to do the correct things, I was basically an agnostic. I didn't know whether or not God existed.

I was excited about starting college. I enjoyed the opportunity to attend seminars and lectures, learn new stuff, and explore some of the things in what I considered a big city (Lexington) via its extensive city bus service. I didn't own a car when I started college. I enjoyed the relative independence I had, and the college atmosphere.

Just as I didn't attend church during my high school years, I didn't attend when I began college either.

However, I generally behaved responsibly. My parents, reading, etc., had taught me well about the temptations many college students succumb to.

I didn't get involved in the fornication and abuse of alcohol and other drugs that many other students did. I knew alcoholic beverages and other drugs had harmful effects.

And I avoided premarital sex. I knew where babies came from and I didn't want any while in college. Also, I knew the only birth control methods available to men were condoms and abstinence. And, condoms were not considered all that effective. There was also the risk of venereal diseases.

A bit later in my freshman year, a speaker to residents of my dorm told us that persons who depended on condoms for birth control were called parents. I felt he was right and practiced sexual abstinence.

In many ways, I was a responsible student. Even without mom to wake me up, I got up and to class on time. I used an alarm clock. My attendance record for classes was probably one of the best on campus.

But, I was too much of a UK basketball and UK football fan. And probably more important, I had chosen the wrong major. I realize that now. My passion was definitely writing, not engineering.

However, during my undergraduate days I took electives in a variety of subjects, including several English courses.

My freshman roommate was my best friend from high school. He went to Phelps High School, the high school I attended until the middle of my junior year. I knew him better and longer than any of the friends I had at Jenkins, though nice guys in my class from Jenkins went to UK. My friend and I had enjoyed numerous discussions on various topics from sports to current events during my time at Phelps.

He contacted me about the possibility of being my roommate. I was pleasantly surprised that he did and accepted his offer. My dad had suggested I contact him about the possibility of being my roommate, but I hadn't. My guess is that my dad took the initiative of contacting him and my friend then contacted me. But that's just a guess.

It was nice having a good friend as my roommate rather than a stranger. Many if not most freshman students didn't know their roommate until they arrived on campus. But in some ways having a good friend as a roommate may have prevented me from taking the initiative to develop more new friendships. And I was more demanding and less understanding of my good friend than I was of my other college roommates. And I was blessed with good ones.

I stayed in campus dormitories all through my undergraduate years. My best friend elected to live in an off-campus apartment his second year, though we remained friends, and still are.

I don't think mom mentioned it while I was in college, but somewhat recently, within the last year, mom told me (I think in a phone conversation which is the way she's told me many things over the years, including much of what's in this book.), that she cried when I moved away to college. She said she probably did it after she got home away from me, and at a time when dad couldn't see her. She said she knew I had to do it, but she still cried. I think that's probably the case for many if not most moms.

I worked in the mining industry during the summer after my first year of college. The work began with safety training, which I think lasted a week. I was probably the worst in the class at some of the safety training, such as using concrete blocks to build a seal, etc.

My number of work days was limited due to a Wildcat strike. Some miners from West Virginia set up a picket line urging us not to work. They were striking over health care benefits is my understanding. I remember driving each scheduled work night to see if the pickets were there.

After my second year of college, I attended a surveying camp for I think three weeks, possibly being the worst student in the class, then worked the rest of the summer as a mining engineer trainee. I think I may have been the worst mining engineer trainee they had. Surveying was a significant part of the work, and I was not good at it, despite my dad devoting much of his time to that field. I will spare the details. I do feel I helped the company in a few ways though, and it was a good learning experience for me.

The remaining summers during my undergraduate college years, I went to summer school.

During the spring of 1980, during my fourth year of college, I caught pneumonia. I had camped out overnight on Saturday night for UK men's basketball tickets, which I'd done before. But this time, instead of staying outside all night, I took at least one break in the car mom and dad had let me drive to school earlier that school year.

I felt colder that night than when I'd stayed out all night. I surmise that the changing of the temperature back and forth that way led to the pneumonia due to the temperature changes weakening my immune system.

Partially due to being out of class for some time due to the pneumonia, I had to drop the majority of my classes. When I returned to school, I saw an advertisement in the Lexington newspaper for census workers, stating there was a big demand. I decided that due to my reduced course load, I had time for a part-time job. I responded to the ad.

I remember going to take the test. I naively thought that was the key to being hired. I learned otherwise. I had expected to see some other college students there, but the others there to take the test did not appear to be students. The test seemed easy, and I felt I would get a job easily.

But near the end of the test, one of the others taking it said something like "This test is hard. I didn't know we had to take a test." Another person said something like, "We have to take the test but it doesn't count. What counts is your points." Another person said, something like "And there's supposed to be a line on here to put a Democratic party official for a reference. I don't see it. What line is that?"

After these comments, the proctor of the exam, red faced, told us to put our pencils down for a minute while he explained some things. He explained that the test was just one part of the application process. He added that persons got extra points added to their test scores for being military veterans, disabled, female, or members of a minority group. Then he looked at me and said something like "And if you're not a member of any of those groups, you don't get any extra points."

He added that it also helps to have a reference from an elected or appointed official, a Democratic one. He noted that the test didn't state which line to put it on, but he then told us what line to list that on.

I finished the exam. When I turned in my exam to the proctor, I was a bit upset, probably more than a bit upset. I told him something like "I feel I got perhaps the highest score in the group on this test and am well qualified for the job. But I don't know any Democratic elected officials. However, if I don't get hired, I'm going to complain even if I have to have that peanut farmer in the White House impeached."

The proctor wrote something briefly, then he asked me something like "Do you want me to write down President Carter or peanut farmer in the White House?" I think I replied "peanut farmer in the White House" and he stated something to the effect "well, President Carter is a peanut farmer or was, but he's actually done quite a lot of things. I notice your application states you're an engineering major. President Carter used to be a nuclear engineer, at least he taught nuclear engineering in the Navy, or so I've been told. I haven't researched it. You could research it if you want to. And I am a Democrat."

I think he waited as if expecting me to say something else, then said something like "Well okay, peanut farmer in the White House, it is."

Actually, some (several?) of those other applicants probably were more qualified for the job than me despite earning lower test scores. And I knew little about President Carter. I am now confident that Carter knew more about engineering (and many other things) that I ever have or ever will. Furthermore, President Carter probably had no idea how the census hiring was conducted in Lexington. Finally, if I had responded more tactfully, the proctor might have helped me get a job sooner.

At any rate, I calmed down. I did not complain to follow up on this. Much time went by and I guess many if not most of the others in that class were interviewed and hired. Maybe they were known by Democratic officials who knew/felt they would do a good job.

But I finally did get a call from someone. The caller asked if I had applied for a census job, if I'd been hired or interviewed, and then when I replied that I had not, the individual stated that was surprising considering how good my test score was, then added basically "well maybe not considering the answer to one question." I can guess which one.

This person stated that most Census jobs at that time, in Lexington at least, were Democratic political patronage jobs. But there were some jobs the Democrats couldn't or wouldn't do. He/she stated his/her title, adding that though it was a somewhat low position, he/she was probably the highest ranking Republican in the Lexington Census office, and in charge of getting many of the tough jobs done that Democrats couldn't or wouldn't perform.

This person told me she/he didn't care which political party I belonged to as long as I was qualified for the job, then mentioned a specific job she/he had in mind for me. I was hired. Individual census records are confidential by law for good reasons. I can't state any details about the specific census records I saw.

I appreciated the job opportunity and tried to do it well. But in hindsight, I was ill prepared for all that was involved in the tasks my job entailed. My job involved supervising and checking the work of some persons conducting census operations in a specific area. I was glad when my job was completed.

During my spare time at college, I enjoyed attending seminars and lectures that were offered at UK. These sometimes featured prominent speakers. Thought-provoking question and answer sessions often followed after the initial speech.

I remember hearing atheist Madalyn Murray O'Hair, Christian apologist Josh McDowell, former President Gerald Ford, former Presidential candidate George McGovern, and numerous others speak.

Several of the seminars/lectures were sponsored by

the Bluegrass Chapter of UNA-USA and/or the Patterson School of Diplomacy and International Commerce. UNA-USA is an organization geared toward supporting the work of the United Nations in various ways. The Patterson School is one of the schools on the University of Kentucky campus. It offers a focus that probably wasn't available anywhere else in the southeastern United States at that time. The Carter Center in Georgia now has some similarities, but a much different approach and focus. Also, the Carter Center is not a branch of a university.

There were lots of resources available at UK that I did not take advantage of while I was there. If I had it to do over again, I could have made my college years much more productive.

My first semester freshman year it would have been nice to get a tutor for MA113, Calculus I, or better yet to have taken a different class. The summer before college, my summer advising conference advisor tried to get me to sign up for an honor's math class, noting my excellent high school grades and my high ACT math entrance exam score. It would likely have offered a smaller class size, a better instructor, and I'd have learned more. But engineering required MA113, so I registered for it.

Just after I finished my registration, I heard my advisor tell another advisor that I'd made a mistake by taking the section of MA113 I registered for. He told that person, he knew the instructor for the course, and he was a very poor one.

The same summer advising conference person had

also told me I was eligible to take a test, and if I got a high enough score, I could avoid taking freshman English due to my high ACT English score. Related to other ACT test takers, my English ACT score was even higher than my ACT math score. But instead of taking the test, enrolled in English 105, which is a bit more advanced than the standard English 101, but still a freshman class.

I was happy about my English decision. But I learned as a first semester freshman a few months later that my advisor was correct about my math instructor. Indeed, most persons in my particular MA113 class either dropped out or failed the class.

One of the few who did well in it told me he had virtually stopped attending this class and was attending another MA113 section with a much better instructor, and urged me to do so too. He noted that we all took the same standardized exams at another location, as I knew, so it mattered little which instructor's class we attended.

This fellow student said he only came back to our class for quizzes. He said the instructor knew he wasn't an effective teacher, and had encouraged him to relay this message to me, since he felt I could benefit from a better instructor. Apparently some others from my class also attended another section for the lectures. Most of those who didn't failed the class.

In hindsight, I'd have done well to take that student's advice, even better to have taken my summer advising conference advisor's advice, and better yet to have changed my major.

I could also have gotten a tutor for certain other required engineering-related classes. But, in hindsight, it would have been a great idea to change my major to business, journalism, political science, or communications. The Counseling and Testing Service, various organizations, etc., would also have been nice to use and/or become involved with.

But the quality of the instructor matters a lot. I was blessed with several gifted ones in college, as well as some others that like my first semester calculus instructor seemed poorly suited for the job.

The quality of a course's textbook matters too, and our calculus textbook seemed to have significant deficiencies. In a later semester I purchased a copy of *The Calculus Problem Solver*, a large volume which offered numerous calculus problems and their step by step solution, as well as some additional information. I found it, and some other books in the Problem Solver Series for other courses, helpful.

A student's passion, dedication, and aptitude for a course's subject matter are important too. My passion, dedication, and aptitude often seemed to lead in other directions than engineering.

During my college years, I took a lot of electives. Many of them were prerequisites for the MBA program. Several others were English classes. And I took some in other areas too. I enjoyed learning about different things. As a result of the extra courses, it took me six years to receive my undergraduate degree. But in some ways, I learned more in my electives than in my required engineering classes.

I am grateful for my scholarship, and for dad paying for much of my expenses as well.

During my 4th year in college, I looked around the Keeneland dorm that I lived in to see which room I thought was best. When I sent in my application for a dorm room for the next year, I selected that room. And I sent my application in early. I knew room assignments were made based on the date the application was received.

After arriving on campus the next year, when the other person assigned to the room, Paul Craft, arrived, he stated that someone else was supposed to be in the room with him. I told him that I had applied for the room. But if he wanted to switch to another room to be with that person, he was welcome to. The other person in that room, whoever it was, could room with me instead. I told him I'd be happy to room with anyone.

And that's true. I seek to get along with everyone. Paul chose to stay in the room with me. And Paul was a wonderful roommate. We roomed together the next year too, and we remain good friends. Indeed, I like to think that I remain friends with everyone I've ever met. I certainly consider everyone a friend.

In a sense, I felt I picked the best room and got the best roommate. However, my previous roommates were all nice too.

Paul invited me to church at least a few times. Then I decided that the next time he invited me I'd go with him. It was a surprisingly long time, but he did eventually ask again, and I agreed to go. I later was baptized and joined that nearby Baptist Church, though even then I was perhaps more of a nondenominational Christian than a Baptist or at least a more conservative

Baptist than that church appeared to be at the time. Paul often went home to northern Kentucky on weekends where his church membership was.

I did develop some nice friendships at that church though. And the church began a college forum which offered pizza and soft drinks followed by a guest speaker and a question and answer session. I enjoyed this much. The pizza and soft drinks were either free or very cheap. A significant part of my small monetary donations to the church probably served to subsidize my pizza. I was probably [blush] one of the top two pizza eaters, if not #1. But I actually enjoyed the speakers, discussions, and fellowship more than the pizza. I commend Calvary Baptist Church for taking the initiative to institute this.

I'd been saying an evening prayer since childhood, and began reading a New Testament then a Bible the academic year before rooming with Paul. But it was Paul's invitation that got me started attending church and led to my joining Calvary Baptist Church later.

In addition to a church, I joined some other organizations while I was in college, such as the student chapters of AIME, ASCE, and KSPE, related to my engineering studies. I also joined the UK MBA Student Association while I was in the MBA program and the UK Finance Association. I confess that I was not very active in any of them though, and definitely wasn't in a leadership role in them. I liked the business organizations more than the engineering ones though.

Indeed, I enjoyed the MBA program much more than engineering. But I didn't really feel called into the business world. While studying with some MBA program classmates, we discussed job prospects for after graduation. I mentioned the possibility of my becoming a paperback writer, similar to one referred to in a Beatles song several years earlier. I was serious about considering a writing career.

I enjoyed international, intercultural things. In 1982 I purchased a season ticket to the 1982 World's Fair in Knoxville. I think I went to it four times, driving from Lexington there in the morning and back in the evening due to the high cost and limited supply of lodging in Knoxville.

At some point I joined the Bluegrass Society of MBAs.

Early Career Days and Return to College

I wanted an honest job that I was qualified for after graduation. I applied for jobs via the University of Kentucky placement service.

My resume was nice. Part of that was due to my writing skills. Part of it was due to resume writing books I'd read and tips from a UK Placement Service person who reviewed my resume.

But my interview skills were not very good. My shyness was a factor. And I had relatively little work experience. Perhaps most important, I lacked passion for civil and mining engineering, my undergraduate majors. And I did not do well in a lot of core engineering classes.

I did enjoy several of my undergraduate electives, including my English classes and most of the prerequisites for the MBA program. I did well on the GMAT test that served as the entrance exam for the MBA program.

I also enjoyed my MBA classes, including perhaps especially the case studies, and group work, including group work on projects in the MBA program such as case studies, etc.

But my passion remained reading and writing, although I was sincerely interested in helping businesses overcome problems and perform better.

The area of the MBA program that interested me most was management consulting. But I didn't want to take on a career with a major accounting firm in that area due to my perception of the extremely long hours and dedication required. And I didn't see any ads for such jobs locally either, and I enjoyed the Lexington area.

Also, though I applied for jobs via the University of Kentucky placement service, and I looked at ads in the Lexington newspaper, I did not go door to door applying directly to businesses. That was probably a mistake.

I saw a newspaper ad for a job with Encyclopaedia Britannica. I mentioned the ad to my friend Paul, and urged him to phone. He did. Then I phoned. I thought it might be a good job opportunity.

And when my friend Paul applied for a USPS job, I went with him and applied too.

I wanted a job I was qualified for. I thought I might do well on the P.O. test and application. And I felt passionate about the quality of Encyclopaedia Britannica.

My interest in reading and my view about the impressiveness of Britannica, as well as reading about the success of John Y. Brown as a sales representative and manager for them led me to think it might be a good fit for me. But encyclopedia (or encyclopaedia as Britannica spells it) sales did not work out well for me.

Sales in general is not a field I think I'd be extremely effective at. Indeed, I've given away more copies of the books I've written than I've sold. I did learn much from that job though.

I eventually was hired at the P.O. I sought to be a writer after leaving the P.O. Indeed, at the time I applied at the P.O., my goal was to be a writer, with that being the second job that kept the bills paid, though I didn't actually do much, if any, writing during my time at the P.O.

My work at the Post Office was a good learning experience too, though in many ways it was very unusual. One event that was especially unusual and almost unbelievable, I discussed in my previous two books. Briefly, several persons wearing dress clothes much different than the casual apparel we evening workers wore visited the Post Office at least one evening and walked around the work area. One of my coworkers asked one of them when persons were to be killed at a Post Office in Oklahoma. The other person in reply asked the coworker how he knew about it, since it was supposed to be secret. The conversation mentioned no date or specific location, but I don't think it was many days later when some persons were killed at a Post Office in Oklahoma by someone.

I discuss the conversation and the aftermath in more detail in my first two books. For years afterward I was followed around. And I received veiled and unveiled death threats.

I've enjoyed playing games since childhood when

time permits. After I read in the Lexington newspaper about it, I attended a Scrabble® tournament at the Lexington Senior Citizens Center in the mid1980s that was open to the public and then became a member (maybe even a charter member) of a Scrabble® Club.

I left my job at the Post Office. I felt mentally, physically, and emotionally exhausted. Many additional unusual events had been happening, though not as unusual as that conversation.

Perhaps I should have moved back to southeastern Kentucky at that point. But I didn't want to, though I visited folks there from time to time.

I don't remember when it was, but I'm guessing it was within a year or two after I left my job at the Post office, as I was driving back to Lexington from a visit to see relatives and friends in southeastern Kentucky, I encountered a terrible storm. It's the worst storm I've ever driven in.

Rain was coming down extremely hard. Extremely high winds were blowing against my car, and I thought I might be blown over. I looked for a safe place to pull over.

Then when the storm was at its worst, I heard a clear voice stating something like "This is your mamaw; come home." Then the voice added something like "It's not just me. I've got Fannie [a sister of mamaw's] helping me."

I thought about it. I saw no logical reason to turn back to southeastern Kentucky at that instant, since I'd just come from there. And in that terrible storm, I was feeling led to seek to pull to the side of the road and park somewhere safe from the wind rather than to drive anywhere.

The voice expressed the thought that they didn't want to hurt me, then added something like "Not now. But soon." which I interpreted to mean that they wanted me to move back to southeastern Kentucky.

I never phoned my grandmother, Annie Hunter-Wicker (whom I called mamaw as I noted earlier in the book), to ask her if that was really her voice. And she never phoned me. But I'm guessing through some form of communication it was her, and she wanted me to move back to southeastern Kentucky from central Kentucky. Perhaps she knew something about the threats and other unusual things that happened during and shortly after my work at the Post Office. I don't know.

Someone told me mamaw was rumored to be a witch. If so, I hope she was a good one, like the good witches of the North and South in the fictional movie *The Wizard of Oz*. She was nice to me anyway. And she was an excellent cook. I still remember enjoying things like her homemade cream style corn, her applesauce stack cake, and her peach cobbler, among many other tasty dishes. My mom is a wonderful cook too.

I do recall on one visit to see her, in her later years, when I first arrived, she was sitting at her dining room table with a friend, and the two were dressed in very unusual apparel I'd never seen either in. I got the impression for some reason that the apparel was part of some religious ceremony, some type of witchcraft. I didn't ask, and they didn't volunteer any explanation.

At any rate, at some point after leaving the Post

Office, I went back to college and took some courses in Communications, etc. I considered going for a doctorate in Communications, but due to the cost involved, the types of courses, etc., I decided not to. I'm glad I went back and took the courses I did though. It was a good learning experience. This was during the early stages of what later became the Internet.

To help pay expenses after I returned to graduate school, I tutored students in introductory Statistics classes. I also tutored some persons in a remedial math class that was similar to high school algebra II.

While in graduate school during this time, I was invited to become the editor of the newsletter of the Bluegrass Chapter of UNA-USA and accepted the offer. UNA-USA stands for The United Nations Association of the United States of America. It's an organization that seeks to support the United Nations and its work.

I enjoyed this volunteer opportunity and getting to know the others involved with the organization that I met. However, as editor of the chapter newsletter, I basically just typed/word processed articles submitted by others that were already of an appropriate length. I did occasionally write editor's comments though.

After I learned about the upcoming first annual conference of the UNA-USA, which was held in Washington, D.C., I registered for it. I enjoyed its variety of seminars/lectures/discussions. And I toured some of the many attractions in Washington, DC also.

After leaving graduate school, I needed to move out of University of Kentucky graduate student housing. It was time to find a new place to live.

Chapter 6: Living in Nicholasville, Then Back in Jenkins

Living in Nicholasville

After leaving graduate school, I moved to Nicholasville. I wanted to be close to Lexington, and the cost of living seemed cheaper in Nicholasville. I continued doing statistics tutoring for a while, then sought another job, while also seeking to embark upon a writing career.

I wanted an honest job I was qualified for. Furthermore, at this time I'd basically decided I wanted to be a freelance writer, but lacked the confidence to seek to do it as a primary source of income. Therefore, I went looking for a job with the idea that it would be a second job to keep the bills paid, while I did writing. Perhaps some companies don't want to hire someone if they are going to be considering their employment secondary to another job, at least for a fulltime career hire.

I went to some businesses in Nicholasville with resumes without success. Some had no openings, and some said they only hired through the Department for Employment Services. Then I went to the Department for Employment Services and looked at job openings.

Many of the job openings required specific experience I lacked. The two honest jobs I seemed best qualified for were restaurant jobs that required no experience.

I applied at a McDonald's and was hired. Since the McDonald's was on the other side of Nicholasville from where I lived, I began applying at restaurants closer to where my apartment was. Eventually I was hired at a Subway restaurant near my apartment.

To reduce debt, I worked both jobs. My regular hours became Mon.-Sat. 7 a.m.-4 p.m. at McDonald's, then I closed at Subway some days. I was off both jobs on Sunday, since I refused to work Sundays due to it being my church day and day of rest. I often took an afternoon nap after church and eating lunch on Sunday.

My employers seemed pleased with my work. Overall, I enjoyed it too. But I was putting in a lot of hours, and had little time for my writing.

Some weeks I worked 80 hours or more, in addition to doing my own household chores at my apartment. Eventually as my budget improved, I gave a two week notice and resigned at Subway. I continued working at McDonald's but felt led to leave there too after several unusual things happened.

I prayed about it, and eventually left my McDonald's job after praying about it. However, I don't feel I tested the spirits appropriately, and it wasn't the Holy Spirit providing me direction on when and how to resign.

After that I tried to be a fulltime freelance writer, using a computer I'd recently purchased. But it didn't work out, due perhaps to my lack of disciplined direction. I misjudged the Holy Spirit in more ways than one.

Several unusual happenings and my inappropriate way of speaking about them led to a series of events that led to my being psychiatrically hospitalized briefly. But I was blessed immeasurably then as always. That time period gave me additional insights into Christianity.

While living in Nicholasville, I submitted an article for *Christian Single* that was accepted and then later published in the April 1993 issue. It was nice to be a published author. And I hope, through the grace of God, the article benefited others.

While living in Nicholasville I also transferred my church membership from the Baptist Church I'd joined in college to Southland Christian Church, where an excellent speaker, Wayne B. Smith was the preaching minister. Wayne has passed on to heaven now, but I still feel he is the best preacher I've ever heard. In at least his latter years of preaching, he frequently called himself "the biggest hypocrite in the world," but that was just one of his many uses (misuses?) of hyperbole.

Wayne Smith was the founding minister of the church, and it experienced enormous growth. At the time I joined, it was the second largest church in the state of Kentucky. His magnificent preaching deserves much of the credit.

The church was large enough to offer a variety of programs for a variety of people. One program I enjoyed especially was a Deeper Life group. This was a group of single adults that met on Sunday afternoons, led by a ministerial staff member, in meetings designed to help us grow more than in a typical Sunday morning small group meeting. It was a wonderful group.

Also, while living in Nicholasville I sold my car, a 1980 Volkswagen Rabbit that my parents and I had jointly bought as a dealer demo in spring 1981 while I was in my 5th year of college. It had taken the place of the 1972 Ford station wagon mom and dad let me take to college during my 4th year of college. I didn't have a car during my early college years, though dad and mom let me drive their 1963 Ford station wagon to and from my summer jobs after my first two years of college. I've never bought another car since selling my Volkswagen Rabbit.

After selling my car, I began attending another church closer to where I lived. I could have gotten a ride to and from Southland which was in rural Jessamine County a few miles from Nicholasville where I lived. But I felt it was easier to be involved in a church closer to where one lived. However, I never transferred my membership from Southland while I lived in Nicholasville.

I considered moving back to Lexington from Nicholasville. And I considered moving back to Jenkins. Mom and dad urged me to move back to Jenkins. I prayed about it and resisted. But lack of success with my writing, financial limitations, mom stating dad was in poor health, etc., led me to reconsider it.

I prayed about it and felt the Holy Spirit stating it would be okay to move back as long as I stayed in Nicholasville until the election. For some reason, I felt that I wasn't to move back before voting though I had been so busy with work that I'd had little time to research candidates and issues to know how to vote. Indeed, all my life I think praying for the best candidate(s) to be appointed and elected has been more effective for me than my actual voting.

Dad and my Uncle Earl came down I think the day before election day, helped pack stuff up, and on election day after I voted, we finished the packing and moved. I thanked them both for their efforts.

They both devoted much time and effort into packing my stuff up, most of which was worthless to most people, but some of which was perhaps irreplaceable, though of little financial value. My writings were perhaps what I treasured most, and my planned writings which were still stored in my mind in incomplete form.

Back in Jenkins With Dad and Mom (1993-1997)

I moved back to Jenkins to live with dad and mom again in November 1993. My goal was to get a job to work at, do some things at the house to help dad and mom, and do some freelance writing.

However, due to my improper reactions to some unusual events, I was hospitalized briefly in a psychiatric hospital a few times and received outpatient treatment during the period of 1993-1996. The first of those hospitalizations occurred while I lived in Nicholasville as mentioned earlier. The others took place during the time I lived in Jenkins.

My second book focused on unusual events, and discusses some of those that happened while I was in Jenkins. I'll briefly discuss one somewhat unusual event that I didn't mention in that book.

That event occurred when a relative came to visit my parents' house while I was there. That relative used the bathroom, and asked me if we had a plunger, since the waste wasn't going down. As I looked at the toilet bowl, suddenly the waste went down, though it had appeared to be about to overflow instead.

My relative looked at me and asked "Did you do that?" I looked at the person in surprise, then the individual added "You did it, but you don't know how." I think I did say a prayer, because I knew mom and dad's plungers were in another part of the house, and it would take time to retrieve one. I felt that God answered my prayer or somehow focused my eyes in a way that made that happen. Who knows?

At any rate, that is just one of several unusual events I've experienced. Some of the others were even stranger. Perhaps you can understand part of the reason why I received psychiatric treatment a few decades ago.

At any rate, I am a firm believer in the power of prayer. I believe the highest righteous power, God, could have answered my prayer and enabled the toilet bowl waste to go out without overflowing the toilet bowl.

While in Jenkins, for some time I visited the Free Will Baptist Church that my dad and mom had joined while I was in college. However, I also visited some other churches in town.

I most frequently attended the Jenkins Christian Church. That's part of the nondenominational Christian Churches and Churches of Christ group that Southland Christian Church belonged to. Southland Christian Church is the one I transferred my membership to while I lived in Nicholasville.

Escoe Robinson, who has since passed on to heaven, became the senior minister at the Jenkins Christian Church while I was attending it. For much of his many years in ministry he had been bivocational, also serving as a teacher. His wife was named Hattie.

Escoe mentioned at least a couple of times in church that his wife Hattie had stated that before she married Escoe, she had "thought teachers knew everything and ministers were perfect" if I am quoting accurately. Escoe noted that Hattie learned otherwise after marrying him. I thought that was a thought-provoking comment. Often we do expect too much out of teachers and preachers.

I eventually transferred my church membership from Southland Christian Church to the Jenkins Christian Church, though by this time Escoe Robinson had been replaced as senior minister by Sam Casebolt.

I eventually felt led to withdraw my membership, and just be a nondenominational Christian. But as part of the worldwide Christian Church I still felt part of that church and all other Christian Churches of various denominations. And even after withdrawing my membership, I continued to attend that church more than any other while living in Jenkins.

I tried doing freelance writing during that approximately four year period I lived in Jenkins 1993-1997 but didn't have much success. Sometimes I wasn't successful writing. Other times I submitted articles that received deserved rejection letters.

However, through the guidance of the Holy Spirit, I feel I did write a nice letter to the editor that I submitted to Letcher County's two weekly newspapers that they published.

I also submitted an op-ed piece to the Lexington Herald-Leader expressing my pro-life views on abortion while making it clear that abortion was a symptom, not the problem. They published it on December 20, 1996.

I also visited the Jenkins Public Library regularly during the 1993-1997 period I was in Jenkins. And at least a couple of times I bicycled to Pikeville to use the Pikeville College Library and bicycled back. On one of those trips I stopped at the Virgie Public Library on the way to check it out.

I also bicycled to the Breaks Interstate Park and back a few times, enjoying hiking some trails there. And on a couple of occasions, I bicycled to the other side of Hazard, stayed outdoors overnight, then bicycled back to Jenkins.

I especially enjoyed the hikes at the Breaks Interstate Park and using the Pikeville College Library. The bicycle trips were nice too. They provided good exercise and an opportunity to see beautiful scenery.

I had planned to move back to Lexington all or at least most of the time I was in Jenkins. And I prayerfully felt led to finally successfully make that move during the summer of 1997.

Chapter 7: Back in Lexington

Back in Lexington (1997 to Present)

In August 1997 I moved back to Lexington. I tried to find someone to provide me a ride to Lexington, since I didn't own a car. I had sold my car (a 1980 Volkswagen Rabbit) while living in Nicholasville.

I eventually decided to make the trip via bicycle. I bicycled four days and three nights at a somewhat leisurely pace. It was in some ways an interesting and enjoyable trip.

Perhaps I could have called on friends I knew to stay with after my arrival in Lexington. And I probably could have called on churches such as the two I'd belonged to in central Kentucky, one in Lexington and one in Nicholasville. But I chose not to. I stayed with "friends" at the Hope Center (a homeless shelter in Lexington for men) until I'd saved some money to rent a room. Then after renting a room for quite a while, I got a studio efficiency apartment.

I took on a variety of second jobs here in Lexington while seeking to develop my freelance writing career. My first jobs upon arrival in Lexington were day labor via a temp agency called Labor Ready, where you work day to day and get paid daily.

After a few days of working for them, I was interviewed and hired to work at a Burger King restaurant that had an opening. I had sought a regular kitchen position, but he said he preferred to hire me as a porter (actually porter trainee would be more accurate).

He said it required no prior training for the specific job.

I took the job, but I didn't like it and didn't feel qualified for it. After a short time there, I saw a job opening at McDonald's.

I had previous experience at a McDonald's restaurant, the job opening seemed more like what I was interested in, and it paid $1 per hour better. The pay was less of a factor than that I felt I'd like the job better though.

Thus, after about three weeks working at Burger King, I began working at McDonald's. I stayed at McDonald's about 2 ½ years. I left McDonald's seeking to devote more time to my writing and to find a more suitable second job, more related to it.

After leaving McDonald's I worked a few temp jobs, then took on a job with the Labor Ready temp agency at a Quebecor World book distribution warehouse where I eventually was hired on. I stayed there about 2 ½ years until I was laid off along with many other people in April 2003. The warehouse closed the next month, in May.

I've worked several other second jobs over the years. Each has been interesting and a good learning experience in its own way.

Furthermore, at various times over the years after I became an adult, dad and mom voluntarily helped me out financially, though I never asked them to. I appreciate their generosity. I'm glad I've never needed to sign up for unemployment benefits.

I've been in my current part-time second job as a retail clerk for over ten years (since 2010). It keeps the bills paid while I continue with my writing. The retail clerk position offers a nice contrast with my writing. As a writer, I spend a lot of time sitting at a computer alone writing and editing, as well as much time alone researching or reading. I enjoy doing that, but it's also nice to get exercise and spend time around other people. As a retail clerk, I get exercise, interact with the public, and it does keep the bills paid. I currently work about 25 hours a week there, which leaves plenty of time for my writing.

I still speak with my southeastern Kentucky accent that distinguishes me (for better or worse) from most others here in Lexington where I live, with the exception I guess of a few who moved here after growing up in the same area as I did.

For those who don't know, there are even different southeastern Kentucky accents. I'll offer a personal illustration. In the years since selling my car, I've rented one numerous times to visit friends and relatives in southeastern Kentucky. On one of my rental car trips, when I was buying gas at a station in southeastern Kentucky, to be more specific in Pike County in Coal Run near Pikeville, as I paid for my purchase, the clerk asked if my car had Colorado license plates. I replied yes, but that it was a rental car. I explained that I lived in Lexington, and I rented the car in Lexington to visit friends and relatives in Jenkins.

As I left the station, I heard the worker say to another worker something like "he may have rented that car in Lexington to come here to visit folks in Jenkins, but I'd bet he spent some time up on Pond Creek growing up, probably going to Runyon Elementary School, from that accent."

He was right. As I explained earlier, I went to Runyon Elementary School in Pinsonfork in Pike County, Kentucky for about four years from the middle of the third grade to the middle of the seventh grade, while my family lived at Stone. I also attended Stone Grade School on Pond Creek for the beginning of the first grade before we moved away. When we moved back to Stone when I was in the third grade, the Stone Grade School and some others had closed, being consolidated into Runyon Elementary School.

I found it amazing how well that store clerk identified my accent. There seems to be discrimination against hillbillies in some places due to our accent. However, that store clerk was just making a comment.

In some ways I'm a bit idealistic. I enjoyed the fictional movie *Mr. Smith Goes to Washington* in which Jimmy Stewart plays the role of a naïve, idealistic senator. Perhaps coincidentally, on one of my visits to Washington, DC, as I stood in Union Station looking out the doorway at the Capitol Building, I heard someone mention me to another person, stating that I reminded her of Jimmy Stewart in the movie. I do feel I share some of that idealism, which I think is a positive attribute. But I am not a United States Senator, and the movie was of course fiction.

By the way, while I don't agree with Kentucky Senator Rand Paul on everything, he in some ways seeks to adhere to that idealism. He is a maverick, not strictly following his party's views. He has been a strong voice against irresponsible United States military actions and wasteful government spending. I voted for him for Senator.

I do seek to put God, the highest righteous authority, above the government in my writing, etc. And I am perhaps even more of a maverick than Rand Paul, though of course I'm not a political official, just a person seeking to succeed as a writer, to help make the world a better place.

Chapter 8: My Writing

As I stated earlier, I've loved to read and write since childhood. However, my writing for publication didn't really get going until approximately the last 15 years.

Even now, most of my published material consists of online articles/blog posts. And I've given away more copies of my first two books than I've sold. But that's okay. I feel that my writing is blessing others, thanks to God. And my second job enables me to keep the bills paid.

I am blessed to be happy and healthy with two jobs I love, quality friends and relatives and neighbors, etc. All that means a lot. And I'm confident that my writing will succeed even more in my future, at least I think that's the indication I'm receiving in my prayers for God's perfect will and guidance.

Since I consider a major part of God's path for me to be freelance writing, I feel it's appropriate that I include in this book some examples of the writing topics in my online articles and a few samples of my writing.

In April 2006 I began submitting columns approximately weekly to a website my friend Paul Craft started called CraftReports.com at his request. I continued doing so until he shut it down in September 2007. I joined Newsvine.com in 2008 and began posting articles, links to articles, and comments on that website.

I also submitted articles to Helium, Yahoo Voices! (and its predecessor Associated Content), and Google

Blogger.

After my friend Paul Craft started a new website (CraftNationReport.com, later changed to CraftNewsReport.com) in 2019, and encouraged me to make submissions, I submitted a column approximately weekly for it as well until he closed it down earlier this year (2020).

All those websites mentioned above are now gone except for Google Blogger. But, if you are interested, you may view my numerous posts on Google Blogger. To do so, just do a Google search for "Blogger 'James Edwin Gibson.' " My two blogs will probably come up as the first two results on the first page of the search.

One of the two blogs contains somewhat personal posts. It is titled "James Edwin Gibson's Personal Blog." The other one consists primarily of opinion pieces on various topics. It is titled "One Opinion: Some Views of James Edwin Gibson."

The personal blog includes posts about college basketball, what Christmas means to me, New Year's Resolutions, and even one about the retirement of a game piece in Monopoly by the game's manufacturer. It also includes posts about certain places, such as Jenkins, Kentucky; Knoxville, Tennessee; Washington, DC; and Philadelphia.

The opinion blog includes several pieces that provide my views on various events in the news at the time the posts were written. Some are still timely.

Those article topics include: COVID-19, border wall construction and immigration, raising the minimum wage in the United States, and numerous other topics.

The opinion blog contains far more articles than the personal blog.

My Books

In 2014 I published my first book, *True Christianity: It May Not Be What You Think*, then a second edition of it in 2015, with a third edition in 2017. I felt that authentic Christianity was different from what denominations and preachers typically taught as their doctrine, so I felt led to write my own book.

Of course, true Christianity may not be what I think it is either, as I admit near the end of the book. But through the grace of God, I feel my book is closer to the truth than the typical Christian denominational doctrines. If so, God and others certainly deserve the credit, for I know I couldn't do anything and wouldn't even exist were it not for God and others.

I published my second book *Several True (I Think) Stories: Can Truth Be Stranger Than Fiction?* in 2016, with a second edition in 2017. That book discusses many unusual events. Most were personally experienced or witnessed by me. It seems amazing how many unusual things have occurred to me or that I've observed occur during my lifetime.

In 2019 I made some revisions to both books, but since most were relatively minor and the page count didn't change, I didn't call the corrected/updated books new editions.

My goal is to write in a positive, constructive, uplifting way about things other don't write about as I'd like them to, in an effort to seek a better world, one united in seeking to do God's perfect will. God deserves the credit to the extent I achieved that in my first two books (and achieve it in this one). I am of course responsible for any failings.

Writing Samples

I am perhaps too opinionated. Many of my articles/blog posts involve opinion pieces. These pieces offer my perspective on various current events, politics, religion, etc. However, I also occasionally write lighter pieces. I enjoy doing both—probably more than most others enjoy reading my writing.

I desire all of my writing to help readers in some way. How much I succeed is for others (including God) to decide.

I've written on issues like global warming, coal mining, New Year's Resolutions, my love of the Christmas season and how even many nonreligious persons love the "Christmas Spirit," and many other topics.

Below I reprint/paraphrase portions of a few of my writings. In the excerpts I generally tried to avoid including pieces that were published in some form in my first two books.

I hope many of you either have read or will read those other books, so I'll avoid repeating much of that content here.

Facts Versus Statistics, Opinions, Errors, and Lies

One of the reasons for my writing is my feeling that what is reported in the mass media is too biased. I discussed that in a June 7, 2020 Google Blogger post titled "Facts, Statistics, Opinions, Errors, and Lies: Interpreting News." I stated in that article that in many cases what "news media, scientists, politicians, so-called 'experts,' and others seek to pass off as facts actually are just statistics, opinions, or deliberate lies."

I wrote "It's important to seek to interpret what one reads, hears, and sees critically to seek to discern the facts, the truth."

In the article I go on to mention that facts are supposed to be 100% correct. Statements by officials are not facts. We should not accept them as facts.

Press releases (sometimes called news releases) are not facts either, regardless of whether they come from a government agency, from corporations, other organizations, from individuals, etc. The press releases may contain facts, but they typically also include analysis and opinion. And they are typically presented in a way that tries to make the source providing the press release look good. Occasionally press releases are reprinted or quoted in the media without the media even acknowledging that the information being provided originates from a press release.

Statistics are not facts either. They can be presented and interpreted in different ways. As I note in the article, "their quality depends on the quality of the data used to assemble them," among other things.

Opinions are also certainly not facts, even if they are my personal opinions. As I note in the article, "When opinions are supported by facts and quality statistics, they can be very helpful. But emotional, one-sided opinion pieces that lack support and/or deliberately distort the available information are counterproductive.

"If you only consider opinions of one group

(Democrats or Republicans?), you're probably getting a very limited perspective."

In the article I also note that errors and lies add to problems. Sensationalism often seems to make the news headlines.

In the article I go into more detail and use the specific example of COVID-19 to illustrate the difference between fact and fiction. But I think you get the basic idea. Probably you already knew most (if not all) of what I wrote in this subtopic, but these few paragraphs maybe served as a helpful reminder to you.

Ten Fun Things to Do in the Snow

In a lighter piece, published on Yahoo! Voices on February 4, 2014, titled "Ten Fun Things to Do in the Snow," I wrote "As long as it causes no problems, I love snow. One reason is that here in Kentucky we usually only get a few measurable snows each year. Snow is a relatively rare, beautiful, winter treat. Snow seems to cover things with a clean, quiet peace."

The article goes on to discuss the differences between wet and dry snow, some safety precautions for being out in the snow, and as promised in its headline, lists ten fun things to do in the snow.

The ten I listed at that time were: (1) building a snowperson (2) having a snowball fight (3) making snow angels (4) gathering clean, fresh snow to make tasty snow cream . . . . (5) building a snow fort or wall (6) sledding with friends (7) hiking and seeing the wonderful beauty of nature coated by snow (8) photographing beautiful snow scenes (9) feeding wild birds, then watching them eat (10) catching snowflakes on my tongue, then savoring them as they melt.

I may always be a child at heart. The preceding list is not comprehensive. Just standing at a window or doorway and watching the snow fall can seem fun to me for a while.

I could probably write a whole chapter about my enjoyable memories of building snowpersons, having friendly snowball fights, eating snow cream, watching the snow come down and meditating/thinking about it, as well as sledding with friends.

Politics

I've also written some pieces on politics. In a February 8, 2014 Yahoo! Voices piece, posted only four days after the snow article I just mentioned, I talked about Kentucky politics. The article titled "Kentucky Politics: My State Is Not Just a Red State" noted that Kentucky historically has been a Democratic state. But it has been largely a conservative Democratic state, and as the Democratic party moved toward becoming increasingly liberal nationally, Kentucky increasingly voted Republican.

But the diversity of the state was illustrated in that article by the sharp contrast between our two Republican senators, maverick Rand Paul and pragmatic Mitch McConnell.

And I noted that our governor at the time was a liberal Democrat Steve Beshear. Currently our governor is another liberal Democrat, Andy Beshear, former Governor Steve Beshear's son. In between the two we had a Tea party Republican style governor, Matt Bevin.

My article also contrasted the different regions of

the state, noting that Louisville was the most liberal, with southeastern Kentucky where I was born and raised noted for its conservative Democrats.

I considered myself a Republican as a child. My dad, a Republican, was one of those people who joked that southeastern Kentucky had "the best Democrats money could buy." In many southeastern Kentucky local races the Republican party didn't even nominate anyone.

As I got older, I decided I didn't care for either party. I registered to vote at age 18 as an independent, which I remain. Each party has strengths and weaknesses, as does each candidate.

Christian Tract

One of the things I've done over the years as part of my Christian witness is give out tracts. Some of the tracts were produced by a church I belonged to. Some were purchased at a Christian bookstore. And I even gave away devotional booklets that I ordered from a ministry (giving them a small donation for them).

But I decided that writing my own devotional (under the Holy Spirit's guidance I hope), could produce one that meshed better with my beliefs and hopefully God's will too.

On a later page I reprint the text from the front and back of a tract I wrote. If it is nicely done, God deserves the credit. If not, I deserve the blame.

If you find it worthy and desire to, you have my permission to photocopy the page of this book that reprints the text of the tract, as long as you either use it yourself for personal use or give it away free of charge, and you photocopy it in its entirety without any omissions or additions. You may photocopy and give away as many copies as you like.

If you do it carefully, by adjusting the size of the print, you can even photocopy six copies of the front of the tract on one side of an 8 ½ inch x 11 inch sheet of paper, then photocopy six copies of the back of the tract onto the back side of the sheet. Afterward, you can cut them apart to distribute the six tracts from the sheet individually. That's what I do.

Depending on your own personal beliefs, you may also feel that my tract isn't worth taking time to read it, much less photocopy the tract. I respect your rights to your beliefs whatever they are. Indeed, I'd probably even enjoy discussing them with you, especially if we can agree to at worst disagree respectfully.

The front of the tract begins with the title "True Christianity" and ends with my email address. The back of the tract begins with a quote from Buddha and ends with a copyright notice.

My Tract   (Takes Up the Entire Next Page)

True Christianity

We may live happier, healthier, longer, more fruitful lives by coming closer to practicing true Christianity.

By confessing our sins, renouncing them, and seeking to obey the highest righteous authority, which I call God, we may progress toward attaining the things most important. Let's seek to always do the correct thing.

For more information, contact: James E. Gibson, author of the book *True Christianity: It May Not Be What You Think* (2014, second edition 2015, third edition 2017) E-mail: jamesegibson@gmail.com

Let's seek to "be good and do good." (approximate English translation of words credited to Buddha)

Let's seek to love even our enemies as Jesus taught.

Let's seek to live a balanced life that includes integrity, loving service, fellowship, evangelism, teamwork, rest, and tolerance for other faiths.

When we speak, let's seek to always be ". . . speaking the truth in love . . ." (Ephesians 4:15, King James Version)

Copyright 2019 by James E. Gibson. All Rights Reserved.

I've given out numerous copies of that tract over the last year or so. And in recent years, I gave out numerous copies of a similar one before revising it in 2019 into the version copied on the previous page.

Pledge of Allegiance

In addition to the tract, another thing I've done is write a pledge that I humbly think might be a positive alternative to the United States Pledge of Allegiance. Even as a child, it seemed somewhat silly to me to pledge allegiance to a flag, to a piece of cloth. However, the flag does symbolize some things. And, I do think even the current Pledge of Allegiance can have great benefit when read and applied properly.

If you haven't enjoyed the pleasure of watching a video taken from the Red Skelton show decades ago when he read the United States Pledge of Allegiance and explained the meanings of the words, as he had been taught by a teacher during his childhood, I urge you to seek to do so. He does a marvelous job.

But I can also understand the perspective of persons who desire not to say the pledge and not to stand for the national anthem. Indeed, our nation has done much to mistreat many groups of people over the years, as I discussed in a chapter in my first book.

Some of the finest persons I know are Jehovah's Witnesses who choose not to engage in certain patriotic "duties" that they consider worshipping idols. They suffered much in Nazi Germany due to Hitler's intolerance of their behavior; many of them ended up in concentration camps; some died in them. I hope no one ever suffers that in the United States.

I first published a suggested new pledge on Newsvine.com in 2011. In 2016 I published a revised (and improved I feel) version on Google Blogger. And in the next section of this book, I print a slightly revised version of the one I put on Blogger.

My Revised Pledge of Allegiance

I pledge allegiance to seek to always do correctly, to seek to always be obedient to the highest righteous authority, to seek to always be truthful in a loving way, to seek appropriate liberty and justice for all, and to seek to help make myself, my family, my friends, my neighborhood, my country, and my world better by improving my own behavior.

I think my pledge is a vast improvement over pledging allegiance to a piece of cloth and to a country. However, as noted earlier, I respect Red Skelton and his reading of that pledge many years ago. Indeed, I share his view on its constructive effect when said and appreciated properly. But it could be more inclusive, more truthful.

My pledge isn't perfect. But maybe it can serve as an inspiration to a better writer (or group of writers) than I to write an improved one.

Two of the Famous Quotes I Like

United States Senator Carl Schurz is credited with stating in the 1870s, "My country, right or wrong; if right, to be kept right; and if wrong, to be set right." In addition to serving a term as a Senator from Missouri, Schurz was a Civil War Union General, a newspaper editor, and a Secretary of the Interior.

Another quote I like is credited to George Washington: "It is not that God should be on our side, but that we be on His."

Our Freedoms

I agree with the quotes in the previous two paragraphs. And I feel that among our nation's greatest assets are freedom of speech and freedom of the press.

We in the United States have enormous libraries free for the public to use. The majority of us have access to Internet service at reasonable prices that lets us access a vast quantity of information from newspapers, magazines, television networks, government agencies, corporations, citizens, etc. Much of it is free.

Yet, I see a lot of "fake news" posted on Facebook and elsewhere, often shared widely, that could have easily been discredited if the person who shared it had checked a reputable news website, done a Google search, or checked one of the websites that verifies postings.

Furthermore, closing some major servers due to an electrical outage, government shutdowns for censorship, etc., could limit or eliminate Internet service. It's great that we still have newspapers, magazines, books, and other printed material, as well as radio and television. Freedom of the press and freedom of speech are crucial to maintaining our nation. We need more, used more wisely, both here in the United States and worldwide.

Yes, we have freedoms, but to benefit most from them, we need to use them responsibly. I hope through the grace of God and others, my writing in at least a small way helps resolve the world's problems.

Chapter 9: The Future and Closing Thoughts

The Future

Only God knows what the future holds. And I hope I am receptive to whatever God desires for my future.

If God feels the best thing for the world's overall situation is for me to pass on to heaven soon, so be it. But I feel happy and healthy. And my current age of 62 seems much younger to me now than 62 did when I was a child.

If God desires me to write more books, blog posts, letters, etc., I desire to do that. I want to do whatever is the correct thing to do.

Furthermore, though I don't feel qualified for a leadership position in government, if God desires me to run for political office or to seek/accept a political appointment of some type, I seek to be receptive to that. However, as an independent voter who lack experience, party connections, and maybe aptitude as well, that seems farfetched.

But, if God wills, I do seek to write several more opinion pieces for Google Blogger and other sources. I feel that many things that need to be written have not been written yet by others, at least to my knowledge. But again God is ultimately in control. And I want the correct thing, God's perfect will, to be done in all things.

At times I've considered moving to a larger city such as New York City, Philadelphia, or Washington DC. I've visited those three, as well as some other cities.

I've also considered moving back to southeastern

Kentucky. I'll always be a hillbilly I think. But I think it's better to be around a larger group of persons rather than somewhat isolated around a smaller group.

I think it provides more opportunity to witness to others and help others, other things being equal. There is much to be said for the beauty of the mountains though.

And I prefer viewing and hiking the mountains to the beach. As you may know, most large cities are located near the sea or huge navigable rivers.

Indeed, I read somewhere once that Lexington, Kentucky is the largest city in the United States that is not located on a navigable stream. That's just one bit of trivia about the city that I call my home, at least temporarily.

Only God knows what the future holds. However, I am an optimist who believes that whatever the future holds, it will work out well in the end.

Closing Thoughts

Thanks for taking time to read this book. Personally, I feel this book is less important than my first two books and less important than several of my columns/articles on websites. Readers may agree or disagree.

More than most of my other writing though, this book tells a story, the story of a part of my life. My life has been a wonderful experience thus far. I've experienced some difficulties, but I omitted those from the book as a general rule, both to keep the focus positive and also because the difficulties typically worked out well for me in one way or another, turning out to be blessings instead of difficulties.

At some point, God willing, I may publish an expanded, updated second edition of this book. More incidents that deserve mention may be added daily as my life goes on.

If any of you readers remember specific incidents from my past that you'd like to have included, please email or write me to let me know. My email address and United States Postal Service mailing address are both on the copyright page of this book.

Sorry, I won't be offering any financial compensation. Indeed, thus far my writing is not very financially profitable even for me. My second job keeps the bills paid. But my writing blesses me in other ways and seems to be blessing some others too.

By some measures, I have not lived up to expectations. After recording my class's highest scores on some sixth grade standardized tests, winning the seventh grade county spelling championship, being voted freshman class president, voted male most likely to succeed in my senior class, selected as high school valedictorian, recording high scores on the Graduate Management Admissions Test, and attaining high grades in the MBA program, I have not attained much career success so far by worldly standards. But I don't mind.

I know I wouldn't want the pressures of being at the top. I read about the stresses, drug problems, suicides, etc., of many "stars." Persons at the top and those at the bottom often face difficulties. I think the middle road is best. Let God lead, and the rest of us seek to work together as a team, with no one at the top and no one at the bottom. However, I often find that those at the top and those at the bottom are the most approachable for various reasons. Indeed, there are sometimes similarities between the two groups. Perhaps some of those at the bottom have great ideas that haven't been implemented yet.

Ruth Stafford Peale, wife of Norman Vincent Peale, is credited with originating the statement that the key to success is to "find a need and fill it." I feel that one of the greatest needs in society now is the need for persons to communicate the truth in a loving way to help solve the world's problems. I seek to do so as I am led.

I feel my first two books provided some pieces in the puzzle toward that, through the grace and guidance of God. And I feel that this autobiography and other writings I feel God leading me to put to paper (and Internet) are part of that too.

Of course different people are led in different directions. Though I see a need for my writing and the writing of others, I realize the world has many needs. I love to read and write. But persons like myself, call us bookworms or nerds or more disparaging terms, are just one piece of the puzzle.

Civilization needs carpenters, electricians, plumbers, general laborers, cooks, cleaners, etc. Many of these careers require no college education, some no trade school education, and each can be rewarding in its own way.

I'm grateful for those who provide and have provided me safe nutritious food, quality water, clean air, comfortable practical clothing, a nice apartment, bus service, telephone and Internet service, libraries, and innumerable other blessings. Those planting, constructing, transporting, repairing, conserving, etc., are all part of the team that under God makes our civilization succeed.

As each of us does our part, we can make this world a much better place.

Thanks again for reading. And thanks for being part of my life. Enjoy God's blessings!

About the Author

This is James E. Gibson's third book. He self-published his first book, *True Christianity: It May Not Be What You Think*, in 2014 (second edition 2015, third edition 2017). He self-published his second book, *Several True (I Think) Stories: Can Truth Be Stranger Than Fiction?*, in 2016 (second edition 2017). He's also written numerous articles for websites, including Google Blogger, Newsvine, Yahoo! Voices (and its predecessor Associated Content), and Helium.

James is a former agnostic who became a Christian during his college years at the University of Kentucky. He holds B.S. degrees in mining engineering and civil engineering, as well as an MBA.

He has loved to read and write since childhood. As a bivocational freelance writer, he has worked a variety of second jobs to help keep the bills paid while fulfilling his dream of developing a writing career.

A series of unusual events/coincidences and the author's inappropriate way of speaking about them led to a series of things that resulted in a few brief psychiatric hospitalizations for him and outpatient psychiatric treatment during 1993-1996. But he was blessed immeasurably during that time and is now as well.

James is a very ecumenical nondenominational Christian who seeks to love everyone. He desires for all persons to live happier, healthier, longer, more fruitful lives and feels that as we come closer to following God's perfect path, we come closer to reaching this ideal, too.

Order Form and Ordering Information

If you would like an additional copy (or copies) of this book, you can order or buy it (or them) from a bookstore or Amazon.com. You may also use the order form below to order one copy shipped to a location in the contiguous U.S. (not Alaska or Hawaii).

On all orders, please add $4 for shipping and handling. Kentucky residents please add 6% state sales tax to the total cost.

Sorry, no returns allowed. Prices subject to change without notice. Payment accepted by check or money order. Please allow 30 days for delivery. Books will probably be shipped from the printer.

If you desire to order two or more copies of this book (or one or more copies of my other two books) from me, please email me at jamesegibson@gmail.com for prices and terms. Or write me at the Post Office Box address below. If you write my Post Office Box address, please enclose a self-addressed, stamped envelope. Thanks!

Please send me one copy of *A Hillbilly: His Search for the Correct Path*, for a price of $14 + $4 for shipping and handling + $1.08 Kentucky state sales tax if being mailed to a Kentucky address (omit the $1.08 if your mailing address is outside of Kentucky).

Here is my check or money order for $19.08 (or $18.00 if your mailing address is outside Kentucky).

Name...
Address..
City/State...
Zip Code...
Email address (optional)...

Please make your check or money order out to James E. Gibson. Mail orders to: James E. Gibson, P.O. Box 54868, Lexington, KY 40555-4868

Thanks! Enjoy God's blessings!

www.ingramcontent.com/pod-product-compliance
Lightning Source LLC
Chambersburg PA
CBHW050434010526
44118CB00013B/1523